P9-DGM-058

INTRODUCTION TO

image grammar

ACTIVITY BOOK

HARRY R. NODEN

Perfection Learning®

Editorial Director	Julie A. Schumacher
Designer	Emily J. Greazel
Image Acquisition	Anjanette Houghtaling

© Copyright 2009 by Perfection Learning® Corporation
1000 North Second Avenue
P.O. Box 500
Logan, Iowa 51546-0500
Tel: 1-800-831-4190 · Fax: 1-800-543-2745
perfectionlearning.com

All rights reserved. No part of this book may be used or reproduced in any manner
whatsoever without written permission from the publisher.

Printed in the United States of America

2 3 4 5 6 7 RRD 15 14 13 12 11 10

ISBN-10: 0-7891-7779-X
ISBN-13: 978-0-7891-7779-7

CONTENTS

CONTENTS continued

Introduction

To the Student

A powerful piece of writing creates an image in your imagination. Compare these two sentences:

> The dog went through an open door into the school hallway.

> Frothing at the mouth, teeth snapping, a pit bull, a 70-pound killer, bolted through an open door into the school hallway.

The second sentence paints a picture in your mind's eye. It turns on a kind of camera in your imagination. The program you are about to study is designed to help you learn how to turn on that camera when you write. You will learn how to use simple grammatical structures to create dynamic passages. As you travel through this activity book, think of yourself as an artist using words as paint and grammatical structures as brush strokes.

Enjoy,
Harry Noden

Painting with Brush Strokes

Both artists and writers are image painters. Both use all of their senses to capture the things they see and imagine. Both look for details in images— images like the puckering lips of a gorilla trying to mimic the facial expressions of a zookeeper or the clod of grass stuck in a linebacker's helmet as he rises from a tackle. The difference between the two is that the artist, who paints, captures artistic images with brush strokes of paint while the writer captures images with brush strokes of words.

The activities in this book are designed to show you how to paint with words. Each one illustrates a writer's artistic technique. Follow the instructions and learn how professional authors paint their worlds with words. Look at the image below.

Some people who look at this picture see only a vague image of a charging elephant and retreating lions. Outstanding artists and writers see more. They notice details such as the size of the elephant and imagine the flapping of its huge ears and the heavy pounding of its footsteps. They see the fearful urgency in the lions' movements, and notice the young cubs scurrying with the adults. Details like these are best illustrated by using grammatical brush strokes that capture the image. Writers often refer to this as "showing" rather than "telling."

To understand the difference, imagine you are writing about a fellow student entering the classroom. You might "tell" what is happening by writing "Sheila was tired." The word "tired" is an image blank: it fails to create a picture in your imagination. Suppose that instead you wrote sentences such as "Sheila shuffled into the room, yawning, her eyes blinking slowly. She slumped into her seat and buried her head into her folded arms." Notice how the description shows and helps you "see" Sheila. Your mind responds like a video, re-creating the image in your imagination.

Author Robert Newton Peck explains: "Readers want a picture—something to see, not just a paragraph to read. A picture made out of words. That's what makes a pro out of an amateur. A good author writes with a camera, not with a pen." This program is designed to help you write from the perspective of a camera.

We are going to begin by examining a list of five basic brush strokes. This list will show you what happens as each type of brush stroke is added to the core sentence, "**The elephant charged the lions.**" The list will also act as a reference guide as you explore and experiment with each technique.

The Five Basic Brush Strokes

Use this list as a reference as you learn to add brush strokes to your writing.

Core Sentence: The elephant charged the lions.

1. Adding an Absolute Brush Stroke

Feet stomping, ears flapping, the elephant charged the lions.

• Another example:

A dozen volcanic faces with fiery eyes crushed close to the window, **fists hammering the glass.** —Ray Bradbury

2. Adding an Appositive Brush Stroke

The elephant, **an angry 1200-pound beast,** charged the lions.

• Another example:

Steve Brand, **a big man in an old ex-Marine set of dungarees,** was washing his car when the lights flashed across the sky. —Rod Serling

3. Adding a Participle Brush Stroke

Roaring a loud warning screech, the elephant charged the lions.

- Another example:

The moose charged him again, **using her head and front hooves, slamming him back and down into the water.**

—Gary Paulsen

4. Adding an Adjectives Out-of-Order Brush Stroke

The **angry** elephant, **monstrous and fierce,** charged the lions.

- Another example:

More tormentors, Buck decided, for they were *evil-looking* creatures, *ragged and unkempt.* —Jack London

5. Adding an Action Verb Brush Stroke

The elephant **attacked** the lions.

- Another example:

The Bumpas women, their lank hair streaming down their red necks, **cackled** fiendishly. —Jean Shepherd

Absolute Brush Strokes

Imagine that you have written this sentence about the image on this page.

> The skydiver glided toward the earth from 20,000 feet.

To strengthen this image, we are going to add a brush stroke called an **absolute**. An absolute consists of a noun and an *-ing* word. Usually, you can add one or two absolute brush strokes to the beginning or end of a sentence. But if you add three, or if you drop these into the middle of a sentence, they lose some of their power. Here is an example of two absolutes added to the beginning of the sentence about the skydiver.

> Heart pounding, arms stretching,
> the skydiver glided toward the earth from 20,000 feet.

Note with this example that the word *heart* is a noun and *pounding* is an *-ing* word. Combined, the two words create an absolute. Similarly, the noun *arms* and the *-ing* word *stretching* combine to create a second absolute.

Writers, like artists, look at potential creations in two ways: (1) with their visual eye and (2) with their imaginative eye. The visual eye refers to specific details that can be seen. The imaginative eye refers to details that are imagined.

Combining both, the artist/writer weaves an artwork. In the example on the previous page, the writer added absolute brush strokes to the sentence about the skydiver, using a visual eye to create "arms stretching," and an imaginative eye to create "heart pounding."

Here is another example of an absolute brush stroke.

Arms stroking against the current, body twisting for balance,
the man struggled to keep the kayak upright in the rapids.

In this example the author added prepositional phrases to the absolutes. "Arms stroking" is the absolute; "against the current" is the prepositional phrase. The author also added the prepositional phrase "for balance" to the second absolute, "body twisting." Feel free to do this if it helps your image.

TIP Think of the commas that separate absolutes from the rest of the sentence as zoom lenses that invite you to look closely at specific details such as the "arms stroking" and "body twisting" in the sentence above. You can also zoom in with your imaginative eye, visualizing details like "mind spinning" or "shoulders aching."

7

Directions for Activity 1

Examine the image below and follow these two steps: (1) Create a simple sentence describing the image. (2) Paint two absolutes at the beginning or end of your sentence. Write your description in the space provided on the next page under **Description 1** (The Gymnast).

Before you write, zoom in close with your visual and imaginative eye. Look at the gymnast's arms, legs, and body posture for your visual image and imagine what you can't see or hear or feel for your imaginative image. Feel free to either mix the visual and imaginative or create two absolute brush strokes of the same type.

ACTIVITY 1 Painting with Absolute Brush Strokes

Description 1   (The Gymnast)

_____

_____

_____

Description 2
▶ Using a magazine image, an Internet image, or one from a book, create a second example of a sentence with two absolute brush strokes. Be sure to place the absolutes at the beginning or end of your sentence.

_____

_____

_____

ACTIVITY 1 Painting with Absolute Brush Strokes *continued*

Description 3
▶ Watch a two-minute action scene from a movie or television. Using two absolutes, write one sentence describing some small part of the two-minute sequence.

_____

_____

_____

Description 4
▶ Visualize a nature scene you have experienced. Imagine the sensory details—the sounds, the smells, the feel of items you touched. Write a sentence describing this place using two absolute brush strokes.

_____

_____

_____

Appositive Brush Strokes

An **appositive** is a noun that refers to the same thing as another noun immediately in front of it. Think about our core sentence: The elephant charged the lions." In this case *elephant* could be described as a *creature, beast, being, animal, monster,* or *mammal.* To add to the image of *elephant,* you could place one of those other nouns immediately after the word as in, "The elephant, a beast, charged the lions." You could also add adjectives to the appositive to create an even more powerful image.

"The elephant, **an angry 1200-pound beast,** charged the lions.

Notice that appositives are set off from the rest of the sentence with commas.

Now, examine the image to the right and imagine that you have written:

The newborn harp seal nestled in the snow.

To strengthen this sentence, you might add an appositive brush stroke such as the following:

The newborn harp seal, a tiny creature with snow-white fur, nestled in the snow.

Directions for Activity 2

Look at the image of the singer.

Now, follow these two steps: (1) Create a basic sentence about her on the lines below: "The singer . . ." (2) Then zoom in with commas after the word "singer" and consider some of the nouns that might be used as a second label (an appositive) for her. For example, the singer might be labeled with a second noun such as *artist, entertainer, performer, woman,* or *soloist.* Use one of these examples or select a noun of your own and build an appositive phrase by adding a few descriptive words. Write it after **Description 1** on the next page.

If necessary, use the sentence about the seal at the bottom of the previous page as a model.

_____

_____

_____

_____

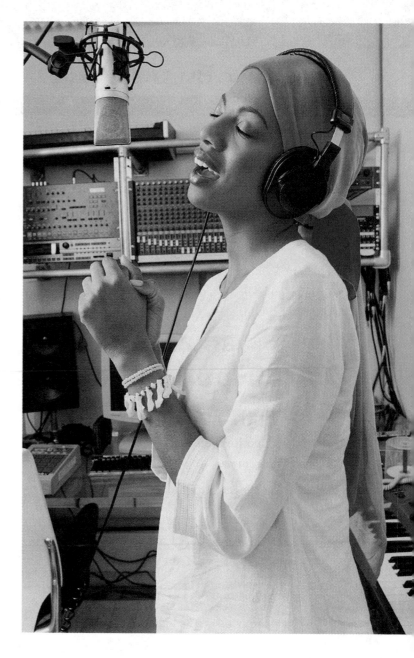

ACTIVITY 2 | Paint with Appositive Brush Strokes

Description 1   (The Singer)

_____

_____

_____

Description 2
▶ Picture a musical event that you recall—a rock concert, a rap session, a folk festival, a jam session, or a jazz performance. Create a second example of an appositive brush stroke, describing one of the performers. Remember to set off your appositive with commas.

_____

_____

_____

13

ACTIVITY 2   Paint with Appositive Brush Strokes *continued*

Description 3

▶ As you watch a favorite television program or film, write one sentence with an appositive describing one of the actors.

_____

_____

_____

Description 4   (Two Brush Strokes: An Appositive and an Absolute)

▶ Picture in your mind the most interesting place you have ever visited. This might be a place in the city or country, or even a place you have dreamt about. Imagine the sensory details—the sights, sounds, smells, and feel—of items around you. Write a sentence or two describing what you see. Include an appositive brush stroke in the first sentence and an absolute brush stroke in the second. Use the brush stroke guide on page 4 as a reference if necessary.

_____

_____

_____

Participle Brush Strokes

The next painting technique, a **participle** brush stroke, is similar to the absolute, but without the noun before the *-ing* word. It can be defined as an *-ing* word (or an *-ing* phrase) tagged onto the beginning or end of a sentence. Here is an example added to our core sentence about the elephant.

Roaring a loud warning screech, the elephant charged the lions.

With participle brush strokes, you can use either one participial phrase as above or three single participles as follows:

Roaring, stomping, swaying, the elephant charged the lions.

Notice how three single participles create a more frantic movement in the image, while the single *-ing* phrase adds specific details to one action. On the next page you will see how to add a participle brush stroke to a sentence.

Imagine that you have written the following simple sentence about the cheetah pictured below:

The cheetah gained on the injured zebra.

To add more detail, zoom in with your visual eye and add this -*ing* phrase:

Leaping with powerful lightning strides, the

cheetah gained on the injured zebra.

Next, view the basic sentence with an imaginative eye and see how a more erratic movement is created by using using three participles:

Trailing, tracking, accelerating, the cheetah gained on the injured zebra.

Here are two additional participle brush strokes created from the image of the skateboarder.

Spinning high in the night sky,
the skateboarder soared over the parked car.

or

Leaping, spinning, twisting,
the skateboarder soared over the parked car

What other participle brush stroke images can you create? Write them on the lines below and be prepared to share them in class.

_____

_____

_____

_____

_____

_____

_____

Directions for Activity 3

Study the image of the gorilla and her baby, then follow two steps: (1) Create a simple sentence describing the image. (2) Paint either one participial phrase or three one-word participles at the beginning or end of your simple sentence. Write your sentence on the following page and underline the participle brush stroke.

TIP Participle brush strokes should be added to the beginning or end of your sentences. When a writer drops one into the middle of a sentence, the participle brush stroke usually becomes part of the main verb, eliminating the opportunity to use the *-ing* word in combination with the verb of the sentence. For example, suppose you decided to write the sentence, "Leaping three feet into the air, the dog shot over the fence." If, instead, you decided to put "leaping three feet into the air" in the middle of the sentence, you would end up with something less effective such as, "The dog was leaping three feet into the air over the fence."

ACTIVITY 3 Paint with Participle Brush Strokes

Description 1 (Gorilla and Baby)

_____

_____

Description 2

▶ If the participle brush stroke you used in the description above was a long participial phrase, try painting the same image with three short participles. If you used three short participles, try one long participial phrase.

_____

_____

Description 3

▶ Think of a dramatic event (a wild storm, a championship game, a humorous situation, a motorcycle race, a family wedding, for example) that you observed in real life or in a film and write a sentence about it. Use either one participle brush stroke or three participles.

_____

_____

ACTIVITY 3 Paint with Participle Brush Strokes *continued*

Identifying Participle Brush Strokes

▶ Locate three participle brush strokes in the following passage. Circle and number each one.

Mud—all around, everywhere. The harder I struggled, the tighter it pressed, eager to
swallow me whole. Soon it was all I could feel, sliding over my skin, filling my ears,
pushing into my nostrils.

—T.A. Barron, *The Mirror of Merlin*

▶ The passage below is more complex because it contains both participle brush strokes and absolute brush
strokes. To find both, try this. First, locate the seven *-ing* words. Five of these are participle brush stokes.
How can you tell? They have a comma before the *-ing* word or they begin the sentence. The remaining two
brush strokes have a noun or pronoun before the *-ing* word. This combination of a noun or pronoun and an
-ing word creates an absolute brush stroke. Label and identify all seven structures.

Men were on their feet, sliding into the water, dragging at the chains, wrenching until
their wrists were bloody, shouting for help, some pleading for mercy from man and God,
others cursing, thinking that they had been abandoned by both.

—Celia Rees, *Pirates!*

Adjectives can add powerful details to a word painting but too many of them strung together make a sentence sound like a young, inexperienced writer created it. For example, notice the amateur feel in this sentence:

The **large, powerful, metal** steam shovel dug into the ground.

The repeated adjectives sound ineffective. When professional authors feel a need to pack three adjectives onto an image, they use a technique called "adjectives out-of-order" and shift two of the adjectives after their normal location before the noun. Observe how a professional author might revise the amateur sentence:

The **metal** steam shovel, **large and powerful,** dug into the ground.

Adjectives out-of-order work like a spotlight, highlighting the shifted adjectives and creating the impact of an almost profound statement. Notice how this works with the core sentence about the elephant:

The *angry* elephant, *monstrous and fierce,* charged the lions.

Directions for Activity 4

In the following activity you will demonstrate the power of using the brush stroke we call Adjectives Out-of-Order.

(1) Examine this image of the kitten and the dog. (2) Brainstorm some adjectives that describe the kitten. Choose the 6 you like best and write them on the lines provided on the next page. (3) Narrow your adjective list once more to just three adjectives and use them to fill in the sentence template.

ACTIVITY 4   Paint with Adjectives Out-of-Order

Description 1

▶ Brainstorm a list of six adjectives that might describe the kitten in the picture. Write them on the lines provided.

_____

_____

_____

_____

_____

_____

▶ Now, select three adjectives from your list and insert one before the noun *kitten* in the sentence below and two after it.

The _____ kitten, _____ and

_____, suddenly realized that he wasn't cuddled next to his mother.

ACTIVITY 4 Paint with Adjectives Out-of-Order *continued*

Description 2

▶ Think of six colorful adjectives that describe the woman in the hammock and list them on the lines provided.

_____

_____

_____

_____

_____

_____

▶ Create a simple sentence describing the woman. Place one adjective before the main noun *woman* and two after it. Then complete the sentence.

The_____ woman, _____

and _____, _____

_____

Action Verb Brush Strokes

We are going to look at two types of verbs: **action verbs** and *being* **verbs** (sometimes called **linking verbs**).

Action Verbs

Action verbs are like engines. They move noun images into action as in these examples: "The car **screeched**. The dog **howled**. The eagle **soared**." Notice how the action verb in each sentence brings the noun to life. *Car* is a stationary noun, a still photograph. "The car **screeched**" creates a motion picture.

Being Verbs

Being verbs are forms of the verb *to be*: *is, was, were, are,* and *am,* and others. These are often used in definitions of nouns as in "He is a mail carrier." Also, they can link an adjective to the noun as in "The mail carrier is tall." Notice, that *being* verbs create still images—photographs instead of films. Sometimes *being* verbs are necessary, but skilled writers use far more action verbs than *being* verbs. Here is why:

Picture the following image in your mind:

The cold wind **was** along the back side of the tent.

This image is like a still photograph. *Being* verbs—*is, was, were, are, am,* and other forms of the verb *be*—freeze the image. Now, watch what happens when an action verb is used.

The cold wind **whipped** along the back side of the tent.

This image literally moves in your mind like a motion picture. This is the difference between *being* verbs and action verbs. When you revise your writing try to use action verbs seventy to eighty percent of the time.

Directions for Activity 5

On the following page you will find a rewritten paragraph from T. A. Barron's book *The Mirror of Merlin* that is pictured here. Many of the original verbs in the paragraph have been replaced by weaker ones. Your task will be to replace as many of the weak boldfaced verbs (or phrases) as you can with action verbs. You will see that there are *being* verbs (*is, was, were, are,* and other forms of the verb *to be*) as well as several other weak verbs that fail to paint powerful images. You will replace both kinds. Later, if your teacher shows the PowerPoint slides, you will see the verbs the author actually used.

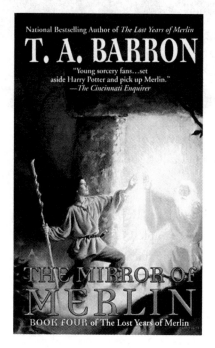

National Bestselling Author of *The Lost Years of Merlin*

T. A. BARRON

"Young sorcery fans…set aside Harry Potter and pick up Merlin."
—*The Cincinnati Enquirer*

THE MIRROR OF MERLIN

BOOK FOUR of The Lost Years of Merlin

ACTIVITY 5 Paint with Action Verb Brush Strokes

The glinting surface suddenly **made a noise**, splitting along a crack. Out of it **came** a long, writhing tentacle of mist that **went** toward the boy. The vapors **were** near his chin, and **were** around his ear, then **came** back. All at once, the Mirror **was** completely flat. Our reflections, clearer than before but more deeply shadowed, **were** in front of us. At the same time, the sound of a distant chime **came** out of the depths, rising from somewhere far beneath the surface.

Replace Weak Verbs

▶ Fill in the blanks with more powerful verbs.

The glinting surface suddenly_____, splitting along a crack. Out of it _____ a long, writhing tentacle of mist that _____ toward the boy. The vapors _____ near his chin, and _____ around his ear, then _____ back. All at once, the Mirror _____ completely flat. Our reflections, clearer than before but more deeply shadowed, _____ in front of us. At the same time, the sound of a distant chime _____ out of the depths, rising from somewhere far beneath the surface.

TIP If you have one available, use a thesaurus to (1) find replacements for the bold-faced verbs in the exercise above, and (2) locate other options for the word *ran* in the activity on the next page.

ACTIVITY 6 **Brainstorm Action Verbs**

▶ List five words below that you can substitute for the word *ran* in the sentence, "The red fox **ran** into the thicket."

1. _____   2. _____   3. _____

4. _____   5. _____

Optional Assignment: Sparky's Sports Special

Sports writers often use action verbs that capture violence in order to entice and excite their readers. Rather than writing, "The Steelers defeated the Browns," they might boost the intensity by writing headlines like, "The Steelers Hammered the Browns," or "The Browns Sizzled the Steelers." How many times have you heard a sports announcer use verbs like those below:

Mauled, Conquered, Buried, Cracked, Crushed, KOed, Ground, Halted, Slammed, Plastered, Popped, Routed, Romped, Shellacked, Shocked, Beat, Belted, Blasted, Bombed, Stymied, Tripped, Clipped, Ripped, Nipped, Sank, Derailed, Jolted, Shredded, Obliterated, Demolished, Busted, Swatted, Pummeled, Scuttled, Whacked, Smacked, Smashed, Slashed, Roped, Bombarded, Scalped, Stomped, Swamped, Dynamited, Smeared, Destroyed, Riddled, Slammed, Toppled, Punished, Zapped, Bruised, Gored, Throttled, Manhandled, Trampled, Tamed, Sizzled, Hammered, Annihilated, Stunned

The news is on the air and you (Sam or Samantha) Sparky, sports announcer, are about to deliver the results of today's sporting events. Create a one or two paragraph news update in which you implement verbs from the list above to describe the results of several sporting events. Use your imagination, to invent imaginary player names, highlights, and scores. Watch the evening sports broadcast to get ideas for arranging and discussing your imaginary teams. Write this optional assignment on a separate piece of paper.

TIP One way to eliminate *being* verbs is to replace them with brush strokes. For example, you can combine sentences like "The dog sat under a tree. He was scratching his neck." Simply eliminate the *being* verb and create a participle: "The dog sat under a tree, scratching his neck."

The Artist's Brush Stroke Palette

Imagine that you are a volleyball player learning some basic moves. Each technique you learn—setting, spiking, serving, and so forth—becomes part of your repertoire, so that as the game unfolds, you use one move, then another, sometimes combining techniques, sometimes inventing techniques. The more you learn, the better you can play.

Writing follows a similar course. The artist/writer creates images in a variety of ways, one of which is using an Artist's Brush Stroke Palette, as shown at the right.

This palette is one of a writer's most useful tools. Like the artist/writer who dips into the palette to add detail to a word painting, you can do the same.

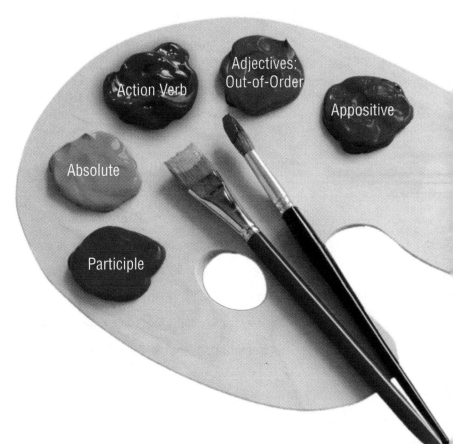

Before you begin painting with all five brush strokes, review them on pages 4 and 5 of this book.

So far you have worked with brush strokes primarily as a method of creation. However, they can also be used as a technique for revision. For example, watch how the following rough draft is revised by adding brush strokes from the Artist's Palette.

Rough Draft

The diver swam silently toward the floating enemy mine. He could see four colored wires protruding from the top. He tried to recall which wire to pull first. His right hand reached for the red one.

Final Draft with Brush Strokes Added

The diver, **a navy seal**, swam silently toward the floating enemy mine. **Peering through his slightly fogged mask,** he could see four colored wires protruding from the top. Hands quivering, mind spinning, he **struggled** to recall which wire to pull first. His right hand, **cramped and trembling,** reached for the red one.

In the second example, each color represents a different type of added brush stroke. When you first begin using brush strokes, you will probably create them as you revise. However, once you become more familiar with the Artist's Palette, you will start to use them earlier in the writing process.

With the next assignment, you will be asked to create a paragraph using a variety of brush strokes. To score well on this assignment, review the rubric on the next page. (Rubrics are guidelines that help teachers evaluate assignments.) For each brush stroke that you accurately create and label, you will earn 10 points. Check your paragraph by using the rubric to be sure your paragraph contains one example of each required stroke.

Rubric for the Brush Stroke Paragraph

Each brush stroke used in your paragraph will be worth 10 points. Be sure to label each technique in the margin and draw an arrow to the example. (Attach this sheet to Activity 7 when you turn it in.)

Absolute _____

Appositive _____

Adjectives Out-of-Order _____

Participle _____

Action Verbs _____

Total Points Earned = _____

Grade = _____

Teacher Comments

_____

_____

_____

_____

_____

_____

_____

_____

_____

_____

_____

_____

_____

_____

_____

Directions for Activity 7

▶ Select one of the two images below. Using all five brush strokes, create a four- or five-sentence paragraph.
Write it on the following activity page. When you are finished, label each brush stroke in the margin.

ACTIVITY 7 Use an Artist's Brush Stroke Palette

Description 1 (Elvis Impersonator or Diver)

_____

_____

_____

_____

_____

_____

_____

_____

_____

_____

_____

_____

_____

_____

ACTIVITY 7   Use an Artist's Brush Stroke Palette *continued*

Description 2   (Paint a Favorite Image)

▶ From magazines you have at home, or discards from the school or public library, or from the Internet, locate one picture that you especially enjoy. Be sure the image is appropriate to share in class and that it is no smaller than a half page of typing paper. Write a paragraph describing the image using brush strokes as you did for Description 1. Attach the image you located to this page. Remember that the rubric on page 31 will be used to evaluate this paragraph as well as the last. Be sure to underline and label the brush strokes.

_____

_____

_____

_____

_____

_____

_____

_____

_____

_____

_____

_____

Collect Palette Samples

Imagine you could magically step into the mind of author Brian Jacques and walk around examining the words and phrases he uses to paint powerful images. Well, you can.

Examine the palette samples on this and the following page, collected from the descriptive images in Jacques' writing.

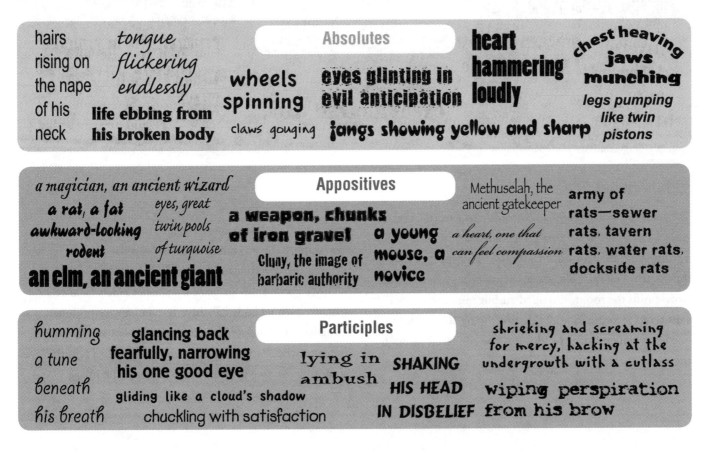

Absolutes

hairs rising on the nape of his neck

tongue flickering endlessly

life ebbing from his broken body

wheels spinning

claws gouging

eyes glinting in evil anticipation

jangs showing yellow and sharp

heart hammering loudly

chest heaving

jaws munching

legs pumping like twin pistons

Appositives

a magician, an ancient wizard

a rat, a fat awkward-looking rodent

eyes, great twin pools of turquoise

an elm, an ancient giant

a weapon, chunks of iron gravel

Cluny, the image of barbaric authority

a young mouse, a novice

Methuselah, the ancient gatekeeper

a heart, one that can feel compassion

army of rats—sewer rats, tavern rats, water rats, dockside rats

Participles

humming a tune beneath his breath

glancing back fearfully, narrowing his one good eye

gliding like a cloud's shadow

chuckling with satisfaction

lying in ambush

SHAKING HIS HEAD IN DISBELIEF

shrieking and screaming for mercy, hacking at the undergrowth with a cutlass

wiping perspiration from his brow

Adjectives

DISPIRITED AND BATTLEWORN

huge and muscular

fierce and powerful

sharp and clear

sloppy and hot

dry and withered

quiet and peaceful

high and broad

Weary and dusty

loud and long

Action Verbs

muttered her charms and spells

drank his fill of the cool, sweet stream water

shivered at the sound of his voice

dragged him from his hiding place

winked and shook her head

vanished only to reappear some three yards out

SPUTTERED WITH UNCONTROLLED RAGE

PLUCKED THE BLAZING TORCH FROM KILLOONEY'S GRASP

seized an iron spike

A Note About Adverbs

The majority of adverbs are -*ly* words that describe the verb. Most authors use them sparingly because they prefer a strong verb that communicates the idea expressed by the adverb. For example, rather than writing, "He **walked slowly** into the room," a skilled author might write "He **sauntered** into the room." Yet, adverbs are sometimes needed when an image or idea can't be conveyed through the verb.

Unlike many contemporary authors, Brian Jacques uses adverbs frequently. However, the adverbs he chooses either enhance an image directly or add a strong emotional flavor. For example, in one instance to enhance the picture directly, he used the adverb *owlishly* to make the reader superimpose an owl's eyes on the image of a character's face. In another instance Jacques added an adverb to enhance emotion. Visualize the absolute "eyes squinting." Now watch what happens when Jacques adds an emotion-packed adverb: "eyes squinting *cunningly*." The adverb reshapes the image.

ACTIVITY 9 Using Palette Samples from Brian Jacques' Vocabulary

Group Activity

▶ Your assignment is to create a one- or two-paragraph description of the two girls singing. (Examine the photograph to the left.) Elect one person as the chairman of your team to help lead your group discussion and another person as a recorder to write down the group's ideas. As a team, review the vocabulary in Jacques' palette on pages 35 to 36. Suggest phrases you think might apply to the singers. You may borrow up to 25 percent of your total number of words from Brian Jacques. Write your rough drafts on scratch paper and use the space below and on the next page for your final draft. Underline any words or phrases taken from Jacques' palette. In addition to using words taken from Jacques, you can create original images with similar grammatical structures. For example, Jacques uses the phrases "legs pumping like twin pistons," and "shaking his head in disbelief." You might create a similar, but original image by writing, "arms waving like a referee signaling a touchdown." Or instead of "shaking his head in disbelief," you might write "clasping her hands in prayer."

ACTIVITY 9 Using Palette Samples from Brian Jacques' Vocabulary
continued

_____

_____

_____

_____

_____

_____

_____

_____

_____

_____

_____

_____

_____

_____

_____

_____

_____

_____

ACTIVITY 10 Using Your Own Palette

▶ Your task is to describe this construction worker using various kinds of brush strokes. This is an individual activity, so you will need to create word images from your own imagination. Use your own paper and the space below to make notes, sketch out ideas, and write rough drafts. Your final draft should be written on the following page. Try to paint with all five brush strokes, using no more than two in a sentence. Label each brush stroke in the margin.

39

ACTIVITY 10 ## Using Your Own Palette *continued*

_____

_____

_____

_____

_____

_____

_____

_____

_____

_____

_____

_____

_____

Fiction into Film

Directors love to make movies out of bestselling novels and popular short stories. Why? The author's words help to suggest screen shots. The following quotes are from novels made into popular films. These samples illustrate how outstanding writers used brush strokes to create scenes that directors tried to capture in their films.

With each passage, notice how brush strokes create a vivid image. If you saw the film created from the passage, try to recall how the director attempted to capture the author's words as film images. Note that the brush strokes are color-coded to identify which they are.

The leader of the pack—**the one that almost got the old man every day**—**leaped** high onto the table and **grabbed** the butt end of the ham in his enormous slavering jaws.

The rest of the hounds—**squealing, yapping, panting, rolling over one another in a frenzy of madness**—**pounded** out the kitchen door after Big Red, **trailing brown sugar and pineapple slices behind him**. They were in and out in less than five seconds. The screen door **hung** on one hinge, its screen, ripped and torn, and **dripping with gravy**. Out they went. Pow, just like that.

—Jean Shepherd, *A Christmas Story*

Ichabod's terror rose to desperation; he **rained** a shower of kicks and blows upon (his horse) Gunpowder, **hoping to give his companion the slip**, but the specter **started** full jump with him. Away then they **dashed**, stones flying and sparks flashing at every bound. Ichabod's flimsy garments **fluttered** in the air, as he **stretched** his long lank body away over his horse's head in the eagerness of his flight.

— Washington Irving, *The Legend of Sleepy Hollow*

Stars winking in front of his eyes, he **grabbed** the top of the hat . . . A gleaming silver sword had appeared inside, its handle glittering with rubies the size of eggs . . . Harry was on his feet, ready. The basilisk's head was falling, its body coiling around, **hitting pillars** as it twisted to face him. He could see the vast, bloody eye sockets, see the mouth stretching wide, wide enough to swallow him whole, lined with fangs long as his sword, thin, **glittering**, venomous.

It **lunged** blindly. Harry **dodged** and it **hit** the Chamber wall. It **lunged** again, and its forked tongue **lashed** Harry's side. He **raised** the sword in both his hands. The basilisk **lunged** again, and this time its aim was true. Harry **threw** his whole weight behind the sword and **drove** it to the hilt into the roof of the serpent's mouth.

— J.K. Rowling, *Harry Potter and the Chamber of Secrets*

And the head itself, **a ton of sculptured stone, lifted** easily upon the sky. Its mouth **gaped, exposing a fence of teeth like daggers**. Its eyes **rolled, ostrich eggs, empty of all expression save hunger**. It **closed** its mouth in a death grin. It **ran,** its pelvic bones crushing aside trees and bushes, its taloned feet clawing damp earth, **leaving prints six inches deep wherever it settled its weight.**

—Ray Bradbury, "The Sound of Thunder"

Authors can also recreate the drama of a movie. If you saw the movie *Raiders of the Lost Ark*, you will recognize this vivid scene. Notice how the brushstrokes mimic the tension of the situation.

Nothing. For a long moment, nothing. He **stared** at the bag, then at the idol in his hand, and then he was aware of a strange, distant noise, **a rumbling like that of a great machine set in motion, a sound of things waking from a long sleep, roaring and tearing and creaking through the spaces of the Temple**. Ahead he saw the exit, the **opening of light, the stand of thick trees beyond**. And still the rolling sound **increased, filling his ears, vibrating through his body**.

—Campbell Black, *Raiders of the Lost Ark*

ACTIVITY 11 Battle of the Tabloids

Have you ever been in a line at the grocery store and noticed a newspaper with bizarre headlines like these:

Astronomer Discovers Planet Made Entirely of Noodles

Zebra Born with Horizontal Stripes

Cowardly Matador Only Fights Rabbits

Newspapers that publish stories like these are called *tabloids*. Tabloids attempt to attract readers with bizarre and sensational stories— stories that are almost always untrue. The goal of tabloids is to sell papers. Consequently, tabloid writers try to come up with headlines that shock and surprise readers. "Battle of the Tabloids" is your chance to have fun by creating your own tabloid headlines, while at the same time learning a few key grammatical concepts.

The first part of the game explores the five brush strokes you have learned that are designed to help you paint images with words. But to use these techniques effectively you first need to review a few basic grammatical structures: nouns, action verbs, linking verbs, adjectives, participles, and prepositional phrases.

Later, your teacher will give you instructions on playing the game. But first, review the following lists of common tabloid words. You will put these together to create five tabloid headlines by using the templates on pages 47–49. Do not share the titles you create until you meet with your tabloid news group. Your titles need to be kept a secret in order for your team to win the Battle of the Tabloids.

ACTIVITY 11 Battle of the Tabloids *continued*

List 1 A Few Common Tabloid Nouns

Androids	Cow Gas	Spoons	Zookeeper	Aliens	Waste
Singer	Vegetarians	Hiccups	Granny	Tourists	Goat's Milk
Psychic	Artists	Treasure	Astronaut	Pit Bull	Pharoah
Motorcycle	Politician	Rat	Alien	Saturn	Corpse
Missionaries	Voices	Moose	Bigfoot	CIA	Mannequin
Amnesia	Hamster	Gnomes	New York	Godzilla	Hypnotist
Vampire	Cover-Up	Clam	Bad Breath	Toad	Amnesia

List 2 A Few Common Tabloid Adjectives

Shocking	Dead	Secret	Wacky	Slimy	Noisy
Miraculous	Ghastly	Toothless	Amazing	Steamy	Prehistoric
Rabid	Hairy	Spectacular	Young	Greasy	Strange
Miracle	Creepy	Stingy	Bizarre	Sweaty	Romantic
Toothless	Gloomy	Bald	False	Giant	100-Year-Old
Rare	New	Toxic	Hot	Cold	Alien
Psychic	Invisible	Ancient	Homeless	Huge	Killer
False	Video	Artificial			

ACTIVITY 11 Battle of the Tabloids *continued*

List 3 A Few Common Tabloid Action Verbs

Found	Sighted	Stalked	Baffled	Terrorized	Visited
Cured	Lived	Denied	Wore	Contacted	Buried
Turned	Claimed	Steals	Uncovers	Collapses	Hatches
Agrees	Finds	Kills	Bursts	Loses	Unlocks
Melts	Swallows	Transforms	Destroys	Shocks	Promises
Weds	Bends	Dies	Vows	Opens	Enters
Captures	Abandons	Discovers	Abducts	Learns	Refuses
Saves	Caught	Kidnaps	Stuns	Brings	Attacks
Sinks	Swindles	Swipes	Escapes	Slobbers	Cries

List 4 Some Common Tabloid *Being* / Linking Verbs

Is	Was	Were	Are	Am	(other forms of) *Be*

ACTIVITY 11 Battle of the Tabloids *continued*

List 5 A Few Tabloid Prepositional Phrases

On Brink of Extinction	By Sleeping on Your Tummy	In a Trance
By Army Marksmen	From Captive Alien	Of Over 200 Tongues
Of the Flying Plants	Of Death	Of the Deep
From Video Arcade	On Her Ipod	With Alien Space Poop
Against Imaginary Friend	Into the Future	In Ozarks
By Lightning Bug	For Dogs	For $500 Million
Of the Ice Man	From CIA Lab	Of the Giant Baby-Biting Rats
Into Werewolves	Through His Nose	On Mars
From Man's Brain	With Horned Helmet	In a Time Warp
With Fresh Manure	In Ozone Layer	With Winning Lottery Ticket
By Killer Squirrels	To Talking Lizard	With a Number 2 Pencil
With a Deranged Chicken	With a Talking Cat	By Using Its Superpowers

ACTIVITY 11 Battle of the Tabloids *continued*

Name of Your Tabloid Team _____

▶ Using the tabloid lists on the previous pages, create one headline for each of the five patterns outlined in this activity by filling in the blanks under the words in the samples that follow. With any of the headlines you create, adjectives are optional. You decide whether or not to use them. In patterns where you decide not to use an adjective, just leave the adjective slot blank, as in sample two.

▶ You will need to make two identical copies of your tabloid titles: one to turn in to your teacher and one to give to your team captain to use in the game.

Tabloid Headlines Copy 1 (For Your Teacher)

Pattern 1	(ADJECTIVE)	NOUN(S)	ACTION VERB	PREPOSITIONAL PHRASE
Sample	Amazing	Gnomes	Found	on Mars!

Pattern 2	(ADJECTIVE)	NOUN(S)	ACTION VERB	(ADJECTIVE)	NOUN(S)	PREP PHRASE
Sample		Farmer	Grows	Monster	Crops	with Alien Space Poop!

ACTIVITY 11 Battle of the Tabloids *continued*

Pattern 3	(ADJECTIVE)	NOUN	ACTION VERB	(ADJECTIVE)	NOUN
Sample	Giant	Toad	Terrorizes		New York

Pattern 4	(ADJECTIVE)	NOUN(S)	*-ING* PHRASE
Sample	Psychic	Clams	Appearing on Teachers' Heads

Pattern 5	(ADJECTIVE)	NOUN(S)	LINKING VERB		(ADJECTIVE)	NOUN(S)
Sample		Saturn	Is	A	Toxic	UFO!

Note The words *the, a,* and *an* are articles and often used to clarify nouns. Include them where you need them, as in the sample above, but don't count them as one of the bold labels in the patterns. Also, depending on the image you want to create, any noun in any pattern can be either plural as in *clams* or singular as in *clam*—each with a different type of verb.

ACTIVITY 11 Battle of the Tabloids *continued*

Tabloid Headlines Copy 2 (For Your Team Captain)

▶ Copy the headlines you created on the previous two pages. Then, with scissors, cut out each example below, trimming them to approximately ¾ of an inch by 8 inches. Give the title strips to your team captain. Cutting and trimming these with scissors makes all the strips appear to be identical to the real tabloid title provided by your teacher.

Pattern 1	(ADJECTIVE)	NOUN(S)	ACTION VERB	PREPOSITIONAL PHRASE

Pattern 2	(ADJECTIVE)	NOUN(S)	ACTION VERB	(ADJECTIVE)	NOUN(S)	PREPOSITIONAL PHRASE

Pattern 3	(ADJECTIVE)	NOUN(S)	ACTION VERB	(ADJECTIVE)	NOUN(S)

Pattern 4	(ADJECTIVE)	NOUN(S)	*-ING* PHRASE

Pattern 5	(ADJECTIVE)	NOUN	LINKING VERB	(ADJECTIVE)	NOUN

ACTIVITY 12 Brush Stroke Golf: A Six-Hole Golf Review Game

▶ Your teacher will explain this review game and provide the needed materials.

Members of the Group _____

_____

▶ Your teacher may have you access images for writing at **www.uakron.edu/noden**. Once you are at the site, go to Options and click on **Images**. Five categories of images will appear. Each category contains about a dozen images, giving you 60 possibilities to write about. In addition, if you return to the opening screen and click on **Online Images**, you will find links to a variety of Web sites rich in images that you can also use for writing assignments.

| Character Images | Settings | Animal Images | Paintings | Abstract Images |

The Musical Rhythms of Language

Professional writers have a unique ability. They can hear the rhythms in sentences. Although we all hear rhythms in the lyrics of songs, the chants of cheerleaders, and the cadence of soldiers on a march, few people realize that these rhythms occur in all forms of writing.

Musical Rhythms in Parallel Structures

Read the following passages and see if you can feel the rhythm indicated in boldface type.

My brother need not be idealized, or enlarged in death beyond what he was in life, to be remembered simply as a good and decent man, **who saw wrong and tried to right it, saw suffering and tried to heal it, saw war and tried to stop it.**

—Ted Kennedy, "Eulogy for Robert F. Kennedy"

The tools of conquest do not necessarily come **with bombs and explosions and fallout.** There are weapons that are simply **thoughts, attitudes, prejudices,** to be found only in the minds of men. For the record, **prejudices can kill** and **suspicion can destroy,** and a thoughtless, frightened search for a scapegoat has a fallout all its own—**for the children, and the children** yet unborn.

—Rod Serling, *The Monsters Are Due on Maple Street*

In his nightmares he can see them. In his mind he can hear them. In his soul he can feel them. Now in earth's darkest hour, **he must fight them.**

—Advertisement for the film *First Contact*

If there are no UFOs, if ghosts really don't exist, if angles are only a myth, then **how do you explain the** traces? **How do you explain the** sounds? And most of all, **how do you explain the** sightings? Beyond imagination lies the truth.

—Advertisement for the television program *Sightings*

Now the only way to provide for our posterity is to follow the counsel of Micah: **to do justly, to love mercy, to walk humbly with our God.**

—Sandra Day O'Connor, Comments at the Funeral of Ronald Reagan

For the sake of those boys, **for the sake of** this government, **for the sake of** the hundreds of thousands trembling under our violence, I cannot be silent.

— Martin Luther King, Jr., "Beyond Vietnam—A Time to Break Silence"

Directions for Activity 1

The drumbeats of language can be created in a variety of ways. Try this activity, which is based on a phrase used by Martin Luther King, Jr., in his "I Have a Dream" speech. Your teacher will divide you into groups of four or five to work both individually and as a team.

Step 1 Select a Topic

Before you create your individual contribution, your group will need to select one of the following topics related to the future. This will be the main idea for a paragraph that your team will create. Discuss the topics and as a group select one.

> Amazing Inventions of the Future
>
> A World Without Poverty
>
> Great Advances in Future Medicine
>
> A Pollution-Free Planet
>
> The Future in a Peaceful World
>
> New Technologies for Better Living

Step 2 Create a Sentence

Once your group has selected a topic, your individual task will be to create a sentence that begins with "I have a dream that …" and follows with one example of what you might dream for in a future world. Your example should be specific. For example, if you were writing about "New Technologies for Better Living," you might create a sentence like this: "I have a dream that all public buildings built in the future will be constructed underground saving millions of dollars in heating and air conditioning costs." On the other hand, an example with few specifics might read like this: "I have a dream that buildings in the future will save on energy."

Next, share your "I have a dream" sentence with the group and brainstorm some ideas that might help the group members improve their specific examples. Then, discuss what order of sentences you think might work best for the paragraph. Professional writers like to use their best examples at the beginning and end of a paragraph.

Step 3 Fill in the Template

Finally, fill in the blanks on the Activity 1 Worksheet with the sentences from your group. Use the following sentence to end your paragraph. **If the world is to become a tribute to the vision and insight of caring civilizations, these dreams must become reality.**

ACTIVITY 1 Feel the Rhythm

Team Members: _____

▶ Copy the entire group paragraph below. Put your initials next to the sentence you wrote.

I have a dream that one day _____

_____ .

I have a dream that one day _____

_____ .

I have a dream that one day _____

_____ .

I have a dream that one day _____

_____ .

If the world is to become a tribute to the vision and insight of caring civilizations, these dreams must become reality.

ACTIVITY 1 Feel the Rhythm *continued*

Bonus Option On your own, create another paragraph by filling in the blanks below. Since the object of this activity is simply to create rhythms, you do not need to research your ideas. Feel free to make up examples to complete the exercise.

▶ Before you begin, select one of these topics for the first blank:

a UFO	a Loch Ness Monster	a ghost	an Abominable Snowman
an Atlantis	an invisible machine	an extraterrestrial	extrasensory perception
a vampire	psychic phenomena	a werewolf	intelligent life on earth
Santa Claus	dreams that predict the future		

▶ With this activity, you may create a serious or humorous version, adding your own imaginative and comic ideas.

If there is no such thing as _____, then **how do you explain the** _____

_____?

How do you explain the _____

_____?

And most of all, **how do you explain the** _____

_____? Beyond reason lies the truth.

Three Ways to Create Musical Word Rhythms

Although there are a variety of methods to create rhythms with words, writers rely most often on three powerful rhythmic devices: (1) literal repetition, (2) pure grammatical rhythms, (3) combined literal and grammatical repetition.

Literal Repetition

This is the easiest technique to both recognize and create. It simply involves a repetition of the same word or phrase. For example, notice the lyrical repetition indicated in boldface in this excerpt from a speech by Winston Churchill during World War II.

> **We shall fight in** France; **we shall fight in** the seas and oceans; **we shall fight** with **growing** confidence and **growing** strength in the air; **we shall** defend our Island, whatever the cost may be. **We shall fight** on the beaches; **we shall fight** on the landing-grounds; **we shall fight** in the fields and in the streets; **we shall fight** in the hills. **We shall** never surrender.
>
> —Winston Churchill, June 4, 1940, in a radio broadcast

Churchill is addressing the people of England. Notice how the repetition creates a drumbeat that expresses his strong resolve. This is an example of nonfiction, but writers use this technique in every type of writing. On the next page you will see a few more word rhythms, representing other genres.

Literal Repetition in Fiction

A new **sickness** invaded Jerry, the **sickness** of knowing what he had become, **another** animal, **another** beast, **another violent** person in a **violent** world, inflicting damage, not disturbing the universe, but damaging it.

—Robert Cormier, *The Chocolate War*

Literal Repetition in Poetry

Half a league, half a league,

Half a league onward,

All in **the valley of Death**

Rode the six hundred.

"Forward, the Light Brigade!

Charge for the guns!" he said:

Into **the valley of Death**

Rode the six hundred.

—Alfred Lord Tennyson, "Charge of the Light Brigade"

Literal Repetition in Nonfiction

Let us let our own children know that we will stand against the forces of fear. **When there is talk of** hatred, **let us stand up and talk** against it. **When there is talk of** violence, **let us stand up and talk** against it. In the face of death, **let us** honor life. As St. Paul admonished us, **Let us** not be **overcome** by **evil,** but **overcome evil** with good.

—William Jefferson Clinton, "Oklahoma Bombing Memorial Prayer Service Address"

Charge of the Light Brigade at Balaclava, Early 20th century lithograph

Directions for Activity 2

Step 1 Choose an Emotion

In this activity, you will work with four or five other students, experimenting with rhythms created from the repetition of one word—a word that expresses emotion. First, your group needs to select an emotion to write about. Choose one from the list below.

Anger	Annoyance	Anticipation
Apathy	Boredom	Compassion
Confidence	Contentment	Courage
Depression	Determination	Disdain
Envy	Fear	Friendship
Frustration	Guilt	Happiness
Hate	Hope	Horror
Joy	Kindness	Loneliness
Love	Patience	Rage
Sadness	Suspense	Sympathy

Step 2 Study the Example

Next examine the passage that follows, taken from *The Wizard of Oz* screenplay. This will be the basis of the template you will be working with. In this scene, the Lion is defining courage with a number of examples. Similarly, you will need to think of examples to express your emotion.

Literal Repetition with a Noun

Courage! What makes a king out of a slave? **Courage!** What makes the flag on the mast to wave? **Courage!** What makes the elephant charge his tusk in the misty mist, or the dusky dusk? What makes the muskrat guard his musk? **Courage!** What makes the sphinx the seventh wonder? **Courage!** What makes the Hottentot so hot? What puts the "ape" in apricot? What have they got that I ain't got? **Courage!**

—From the film script *The Wizard of Oz*

Step 3 Choose Characters to Illustrate the Emotion

After your team has decided on an emotion, brainstorm ideas for types of people and animals that might work to illustrate your emotion. For example, if the emotion is boredom, you might create sentences like those below, using a dog, a groundhog, and a cat. (Note: the red boldfaced items will be part of a later bonus option.)

> **Boredom! What makes** my dog Rex sleep on the couch all day, **waiting for the slightest noise to bark at? Boredom! What makes** the groundhog, **a twenty-pound weed-eater,** spend five months hibernating in a mud hole? **Boredom! What makes** an alley cat, **his mouth yawning,** only sniff as a mouse tiptoes past his whiskers? **Boredom!**

Then as a team, create the first sentence of your paragraph and fill in the blanks under "Group Paragraph" as shown in Activity 2 on the next page.

Finally, you and each member of your group will need to create one example— a sentence that describes what your emotion does. Enter your example in the blanks for Activity 2 on pages 61 and 62 and complete your group paragraph when you next meet.

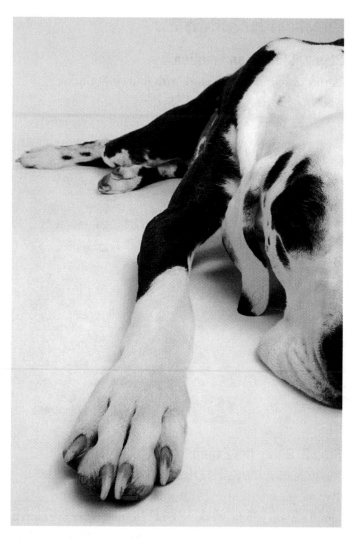

ACTIVITY 2 Literal Repetitions with a Noun

Team Members: _____

Your Emotion: _____! What makes the _____

_____ ?

▶ As a team, fill in the blanks below that begin the paragraph:

_____! What makes a _____ out of a _____ ?

▶ Next fill in all the blanks below, using your phrase and phrases from each of your team members.

Group Paragraph:

_____! What makes a _____

_____ ?

_____! What makes the _____

_____ ?

ACTIVITY 2 Literal Repetitions with a Noun *continued*

_____! What makes the _____

_____?

_____! What makes a _____

_____?

▶ Add one additional example if needed for a group of five:

_____! What makes the _____

_____?

_____!

▶ You can end with one of the examples from your group, or you can end with the statement below if it works for your emotion:

What makes the Hottentot so hot? What puts the "ape" in apricot? What have they got that I ain't got? _____!

Bonus Option Return to the passage on page 60 and examine the examples of brush strokes in red type. Earn 5 bonus points for each example of any type of brush stroke you include in your "What makes . . ." sentence. Label the type of brush stroke in the margin. (Maximum points = 15.)

Repetition of Words and Sounds in Poetry and Song Lyrics

Poets and songwriters are fascinated by the power of repetition and often construct poems and song lyrics using not only literal repetition but also repetitions of rhyme. Here are examples by two well-known poets. Notice the repeated words in blue and the repeated sounds in red.

There Is Another Sky

There is another sky,

Ever serene and **fair**,

And **there is another** sunshine,

Though it be darkness **there**;

Never mind faded forests, Austin,

Never mind silent fields—

Here is a little forest,

Whose leaf is ever **green**;

Here is a brighter garden,

Where not a frost has **been**;

In its unfading flowers

I hear the bright bee **hum**:

Prithee, my brother,

Into my garden **come**!

—Emily Dickinson

The Abominable Snowman

I've never seen an abominable snowman,

I'm hoping not to **see one**,

I'm also **hoping**, if I do,

That it will be a **wee one**.

—Ogden Nash

Woman Walking in an Exotic Forest, Henri Rousseau, 1905

Songwriters also rely on repetition to create powerful rhythms in their music. Many times the repetition comes in a repeated chorus that includes the title of the song. Here is an example from Trisha Yearwood's song, "She's In Love with the Boy."

Her daddy says

He ain't worth a **lick**

When it comes to brains

He got the short end of the **stick**

But Katie's young

and, man, she just don't **care,**

She'd follow Tommy **anywhere**

She's in love with the boy

She's in love with the boy

She's in love with the boy

And even if they have to run **away**

She's gonna marry that boy **someday**

In many blues lyrics, a sentence is repeated with a different sentence concluding a three sentence stanza. Here is an example taken from the blues standard "Good Morning Blues" written by a blues singer known as Leadbelly.

Good morning blues. Blues how do you do?

Good morning blues. Blues how do you do?

We're doing all right—mostly thanks to **you.**

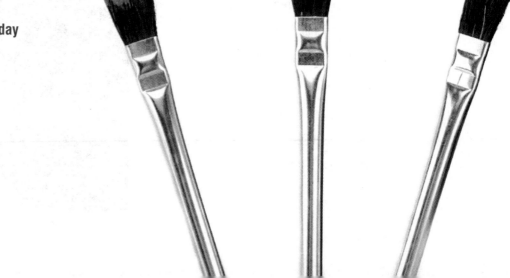

ACTIVITY 3 Repetition of Words and Sounds in Poetry and Songs

▶ Locate repeated words and sounds in two genres: a poem and a song. Be sure the lines or lyrics are appropriate for sharing in class. Then copy below (1) three or four lines of poetry containing repeated words and repeated sounds, and (2) three or four lines of repeated words and sounds from a song. Each example only needs to be a few lines taken from the entire poem and song. Be prepared to read your examples aloud. Copy your examples on this and the following page.

Note If you need help locating a poem to use for this activity, go to the Web and search Google or the Internet for "famous poems." Similarly, insert "song lyrics" and the name of your favorite singer into Google to locate song lyrics.

Poem _____

Poet _____

Example _____

_____

_____

_____

_____

_____

_____

ACTIVITY 3 Repetition of Words and Sounds in Poetry and Songs

continued

Song Title_____

Singer_____

Example _____

_____

_____

_____

_____

_____

_____

_____

_____

_____

_____

Bonus Option Bring a recording of the song or poem to share with the class.

Literal Repetitions with Clauses and Phrases

You can also produce rhythms by repeating the same subordinate conjunction, relative pronoun, or preposition. Review the following lists. These words are the drumsticks that beat out rhythms of clauses and phrases:

Subordinate Conjunctions

after	although	as	as if
because	before	even if	even though
if	since	so that	unless
until	whatever	when	whenever
where	wherever	whether	whichever
while			

Prepositions

about	above	across	after
against	along	amid	around
at	before	below	beneath
beside	between	beyond	by
down	for	from	in
into	like	near	of
on	onto	outside	over
through	to	toward	under
underneath	until	with	without

Relative Pronouns

that	who	whoever	which
whichever	whose		

Here and on the following page are some examples of repetition using a subordinate conjunction, a relative pronoun, and a preposition to create rhythms.

A Repeated Subordinate Conjunction

ARAGORN:

I see in your eyes the same fear that would take the heart of me. A day may come **when** the courage of men fails, **when** we forsake our friends and break all bonds of fellowship, …**when** the age of men comes crashing down, but it is not this day. This day we fight!

—From the screenplay *The Lord of the Rings: The Return of the King*

A Repeated Preposition

66 is the path of a people in flight, refugees from dust and shrinking land, **from** the thunder of tractors and shrinking ownership, **from** the desert's slow northward invasion, **from** the twisting winds that howl up out of Texas, **from** the floods that bring no richness to the land and steal what little richness is there. **From** all of these the people are in flight, and they come into 66 **from** the tributary side roads, **from** the wagon tracks and the rutted country roads. 66 is the mother road, the road of flight.

—John Steinbeck, *The Grapes of Wrath*

A Repeated Relative Pronoun

He was a wealthy businessman **who** worked with leather as a glover and tanner, **who** served with dignity as an alderman and mayor, and **who** in hard times lost almost everything he owned, barely managing to keep his house. He was William Shakespeare's father.

Look at the image of the ice mountain climber on the next page and notice how the descriptive sentence creates a rhythm with the word *although*.

Although a horrendous fall once broke one of his ribs and an ankle, **although** surgery left him weak and disabled for months, **although** his wife and two children protested, Mark decided to challenge the ice mountain one more time.

Directions for Activities 4 and 5

Use the images below to create two passages. For the image of the skier, repeat one subordinate conjunction of your choice and complete the template for Activity 4. For Activity 5, focus on the female volleyball player, and use the relative pronoun *who* to create rhythm.

ACTIVITY 4 Rhythms Using a Subordinate Conjunction

▶ Choose a subordinate conjunction from the list on page 67. Write it on each of the three short blanks. Then complete the clauses on the longer blanks. Review the sentence on page 69 about the mountain climber if necessary.

_____   _____,

_____   _____,

_____   _____,

the skier believed he could make the jump.

ACTIVITY 5 Rhythms Using a Relative Pronoun

Unknown to her amateur opponents, she was a former Olympic champion **who** _____

_____,

who _____,

and **who** _____.

So in this beachside pickup match, she easily nailed the winning spike.

71

ACTIVITY 6 Creating Rhythms with a Repeated Preposition

▶ Examine the image of the crumbling cabin and complete the prepositional template.

The abandoned cabin was dilapidated beyond repair with

_____

_____,

with _____

_____

_____,

and with _____

_____

_____.

Bonus Option Locate an interesting photo from a magazine and create a paragraph using repetitions with either a subordinate conjunction, a relative pronoun, or a preposition. Attach the image to this sheet.

Pure Grammatical Rhythms

Notice how each of the following passages creates a rhythm without any literal repetition. These rhythms are the most difficult to detect since no repeated word or phrase alerts you to the pattern.

Let every nation know, whether it wishes us well or ill, that we shall **pay any price, bear any burden, meet any hardship, support any friend, oppose any foe** to assure the survival and the success of liberty.

—John F. Kennedy, Inaugural Address

Duty, Honor, Country . . . They are your rallying points: **to build courage when courage** seems to fail; **to regain faith when** there seems to be little cause for **faith; to create hope when hope** becomes forlorn.

—General Douglas MacArthur, "Thayer Award Acceptance Address"

ELIZABETH:

It's a pirate medallion.

BARBOSSA:

And we **took 'em** all. We **spent 'em** and **traded 'em** and **frittered 'em** away.

—From the film script *Pirates of the Caribbean: The Curse of the Black Pearl*

Faster than a speeding bullet! More powerful than a locomotive! Able to leap tall buildings with a single bound! Look! Up in the sky! **It's a bird! It's a plane! It's Superman!**

—Introduction to the television series *Adventures of Superman*

ACTIVITY 7 Grammatical Rhythms with Nouns and Adjectives

Be one of **the few, the proud, the Marines.**

—Advertisement for the Marine Corps

In the advertisement above the writer draws you into a rhythm with "the few, the proud, the Marines." Try to imitate this rhythm by completing an ad for an occupation that you respect or admire. Select one of these:

artists	firefighters	police officers	politicians	singers	musicians
scientists	explorers	teachers	hunters	naturalists	athletes
writers	actors	doctors	astronauts	farmers	builders

If you wish to be more specific, you can use a subcategory. For example, instead of "athletes," you might choose "NFL quarterbacks." Instead of "writers," you might use screenwriters, and so forth.

Begin by brainstorming some adjectives to describe your selected occupation. For example Marines could be described with adjectives such as *courageous, fearless, daring, heroic,* or *valiant.* Using two of these words you might create the sentence, "Be one of the fearless, the heroic, the Marines." Create your own advertisement by filling in the template below. Be positive.

Be one of the _____, the _____, the _____.

ACTIVITY 8 Grammatical Rhythms with Participle Brush Strokes

▶ Look at the image of the boy and deer and write a description of it. Brainstorm some ideas using this list of participles to spark your imagination. You can write from either the deer's or the boy's viewpoint. Use your visual and imaginative eye to create a rhythm using **-ing** participles. The following list may help spark your imagination.

detecting	seeing	staring	gazing
gaping	glancing	watching	examining
studying	surveying	noticing	spotting
wondering	hoping	questioning	disbelieving
deciding	considering	expecting	choosing
wishing	bracing	wanting	moving
sniffing	smiling	breathing	listening
stirring			

Note that some participles work for the perspective of the boy; others, for the deer. Select your perspective and complete one of the following two templates.

75

ACTIVITY 8 Grammatical Rhythms with Participle Brush Strokes

continued

Template from the Deer's Perspective

The young deer paused, (*-ing* phrase) _____

_____ ,

(*-ing* phrase) _____

(*-ing* phrase) _____

_____ .

Template from the Boy's Perspective

The young boy paused, (*-ing* phrase) _____

_____ ,

(*-ing* phrase) _____

(*-ing* phrase) _____

_____ .

Bonus Option Complete both templates.

ACTIVITY 9 Grammatical Rhythms with Participles and Prepositions

▶ Here are some prepositions to consider:

above	across	against	along	around
behind	below	beneath	beside	between
beyond	by	down	from	in
into	near	off	on	onto
over	past	through	to	toward
toward	under	upon	with	within

▶ Look at the example below and note how the participle and preposition combine to create a rhythm.

The water moved with incredible force, **cascading down** a hundred-foot drop, **plunging into** a violent whirlpool, and **splashing over** the shoreline rocks.

▶ Now complete the template.

	(-*ing* participle)	(preposition)	(complete the image)

The water moved with incredible force, _____ _____ _____,

_____ _____ _____,

_____ _____ _____,

77

Combined Literal and Grammatical Repetition

This technique creates rhythm by combining repeated words or phrases with repeated grammatical structures. The repeated structures may be any type: nouns, verbs, prepositional phrases, participles, absolutes, appositives, clauses, and so on. In the examples that follow, literal repetitions are indicated in blue and grammatical repetitions are shown in red.

Screenplays

PROF SNAPE:

I can teach you how to bewitch the mind and ensnare the senses; I can tell you how to bottle fame, brew glory, and even put a stopper in death.

—From the film script *Harry Potter and the Sorcerer's Stone*

Nonfiction

Duty, Honor, Country: Those three hallowed words reverently dictate what you ought to be, what you can be, what you will be. They are your rallying points: to build courage when courage seems to fail; to regain faith when there seems to be little cause for faith; to create hope when hope becomes forlorn.

—General Douglas MacArthur, "Thayer Award Acceptance Address"

Fiction

It was the best of times; it was the worst of times. It was the age of wisdom; it was the age of foolishness. It was the epoch of disbelief; it was the epoch of incredulity. It was the season of Light; it was the season of Darkness. It was the spring of hope; it was the winter of despair.

—Charles Dickens, *A Tale of Two Cities*

ACTIVITY 10 # Creating Rhythms with Combined Literal and Grammatical Repetition

Pirate Ship, Kurt Miller

▶ Examine the image of the pirate ship and brainstorm examples of each of the following that might describe it. Then write sentences using these words in sentences on the next page.

Sounds _____

_____

_____

Smells _____

_____

_____

Sights _____

_____

_____

ACTIVITY 10 Creating Rhythms with Combined
Literal and Grammatical Repetition *continued*

I knew the pirate ship was sinking. I could hear the _____

_____

_____ .

I could smell the _____

_____

_____ .

But most of all, I could see _____

_____

_____ .

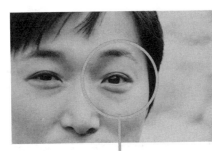

Specific Details:
The Close-Up Power of the Zoom Lens

A noted explorer was invited to Harvard to tell of his adventures with a primitive group of natives on a little-known tropical island.

"I encountered a savage civilization," he explained. "The natives were so barbaric that they loved eating the embryos of certain animals. Often, as they ate the embryos, they would devour slices from the bellies of other dead creatures. To go with this meal, they would grind grass seed into a paste, burn it over a fire, smear it with a slimy substance extracted from the mammary fluid of still other animals, and then eat that as well."

The audience was horrified by such primitive barbarism. "What kind of weird society was this?" one man asked.

"Well, judge for yourself," the explorer said. "What I've been describing, of course, is a breakfast of bacon, eggs, and buttered toast."

This story illustrates how selecting different words to describe the same objects can create radically different images. Eating a breakfast of bacon, eggs, and buttered toast evokes an image that isn't nearly as disturbing as eating embryos, belly slices, and mammary fluid.

Abstract and Specific Words

The power of a word to create an image depends on whether that word is more abstract or more specific. Highly abstract words are image blanks—words you can't picture in your mind. Because abstract words often label an extremely large collection of ideas, they can't be captured with a simple image. For example, the abstract word *freedom* is an important idea, but it doesn't paint a specific image. Each person who hears the word connects it with a variety of different images and ideas. No common picture emerges. By contrast, think of the word *eagle*. It creates a similar image in the minds of most people and therefore can be considered specific.

Compare the images created by each of the paired words below. Notice how much easier it is to *see* the specific words.

Abstract Words	Specific Words
beast	alligator
food	spaghetti
bird	robin
injury	broken wrist

Often, you can strengthen your writing by zooming in for a close-up image. Read the following sentence and try to picture it in your mind:

> The **people** watched the **water** splash against **something**.

As you try to visualize this, your mind might create an image of anything from three tourists watching a leaky water fountain to a group of fishermen examining the currents of a river. The words *people, water,* and *something* are abstract. Now, picture the following sentence:

> The **two surfers** watched the **twenty-foot waves** splash against the **breakwall.**

Although the image in your mind will not be identical to others reading the same sentence, it will be much closer than the first sentence we examined. Activities 1 and 2 that follow are designed to help you develop your own zoom lens.

ACTIVITY 1 Finding Specific Images

▶ The following list contains several matching words that describe the same object. One word is specific and the other is abstract. Circle each specific word.

Matching Pairs

1 car   Toyota Corolla

2 shuffled   went

3 Tyrannosaurus rex   animal

4 whispered   said

5 stream   Turtle Creek

▶ For the list below, circle the more specific words. These are not paired as in numbers 1-5 above.

6 Manny's strawberry ice cream

7 store

8 Count Dracula's castle

9 instrument

10 fruit

11 Vasque hiking boots

12 Grace L. Ferguson Airline and Screen Door Company

TIP When deciding whether or not a word is specific, try to zoom in to see if there are a variety of types that come to mind. For example, in the first matching pair, did you ask yourself, "Are there a number of different types of cars?" If the answer was "yes," you could then zoom in and imagine that the car is one specific type like a Toyota Corolla, a Ford Explorer, or a Jaguar XK8.

ACTIVITY 2 Creating Specific Images

▶ With each of the following **boldfaced** words or phrases, create a specific example that might be used in its place.

1 Antonio was reading **a magazine**.

Antonio was reading _____ .

2 Tonya listened to the lyrics of **a song**.

Tonya listened to the lyrics of _____ .

3 Of all the evening television shows, Rick's favorite is **a comedy**.

Of all the evening television shows,

Rick's favorite is _____ .

4 Tyrone's program was signed by **a rock star**.

Tyrone's program was signed

by _____ .

5 Of all the places to shop, Carmela liked **one store** the best.

Of all the places to shop, Carmela liked _____

_____ the best.

As Ralph Fletcher explains, "Writing becomes beautiful when it becomes specific." Notice the beauty and power of the images as these excerpts from well-known authors demonstrate.

An abstract statement might read like this: Grandma woke us early. Author Richard Peck described a similar event, but with more specific images, in his book *A Long Way from Chicago*:

> At five the next morning Grandma was at the foot of the stairs, banging a spoon against a pan.

An abstract statement might read like this: Three-year-old Gerald heard a sound and saw a fire. Author Sharon Draper described a similar event, but with more specific images, in her book *Forged by Fire*:

> Three-year-old Gerald heard a loud whoosh and then he turned in terror to see the whole window covered with harsh red flames that crawled and licked and jumped along the windowsill.

Another abstract statement might read: Aunt Sooze didn't spend Christmas with us this year. She went to a festival. Author Brigid Lowry described a similar event, but with more specific images, in her book *Things You Either Hate or Love*:

> My Aunt Sooze didn't spend Christmas with us this year. She went to a hippie festival at Byron Bay to learn Tibetan goat horn carving and other useful stuff.

Paint by Zooming and Layering

Adding specific images improves writing. But how do authors accomplish this? There are two ways to create specific details: (1) by using an imaginary zoom lens to see close-up details and describing them with specific nouns and verbs, and (2) by layering specific details with the brush strokes that you learned about in Section 1 and prepositional phrases. Let's examine how this works. The image at the right is described below. The description is an example of a weak rough draft that contains several abstract words and no brush strokes.

Weak Rough Draft

Down the steep **hill** the **man went**. The **wind moved** him forward and **put** him above the **rocks**. Suddenly, where he **was** to land, the clouds **went** over the **place**, and the **man was** afraid.

To revise the passage and make it more powerful, a skilled writer might begin by "zooming" in on nouns shown in blue and verbs printed in red. Watch how specifics change the images.

Zooming in on Nouns

Down the steep **slope** the **paraglider** went. The **updraft** moved him forward and put him above the jagged **peaks**. Suddenly, where he was to land, the **clouds** went over the **ledge**, and the **paraglider** was afraid.

Note that the word *clouds* was not replaced. When you find a noun or verb that you can't replace, it will usually already be specific. The only way to make clouds more specific would be to use little known scientific classifications such as *cumulonimbus, altocumulus, stratocumulus,* and so forth. Many scientific terms are specific. In fact, an old joke illustrates the problem with scientific terms.

The doctor said, "You have seborrheic dermatitis."
"Oh no! How long will I live?" asked the patient.
The doctor replied, "Hard to tell. But, seborrheic dermatitis is another word for dandruff."

Zooming in on Verbs

Down the steep **slope** the **paraglider sprinted**. The **updraft thrust** him forward and **lifted** him above the jagged **peaks**. Suddenly, where he **had hoped** to land, the **clouds cloaked** the **ledge**, and the **paraglider panicked**.

Sometimes it is difficult to find the right noun or verb. If this happens to you, use a thesaurus, a book that lists similar words that are often more specific. For example, the word "ran" in a thesaurus brings up these other word choices: *sprinted, dashed, jogged, scuttled, darted, scurried, rushed, raced, tore, rushed, galloped,* and many more.

Similarly, for the word "storm," a thesaurus brings up these other words: *hurricane, tornado, gale, squall, rainstorm, snowstorm, blizzard, thunderstorm, typhoon,* and *downpour.* It creates a very different image if you describe "Uncle Goober going for a walk in a storm," versus "Uncle Goober going for a walk in a hurricane."

Create Interesting Images

In the visual eye of a reader, nouns flash slide shows of still images and verbs inject the action of movies. Sometimes you can stimulate ideas by using a device developed by poet Natalie Goldberg. Goldberg suggests making two lists of words—one list of a wide variety of nouns, the other list of verbs used in a specific occupation. To illustrate, she gives these two lists as examples:

Nouns

lilacs	horse	cats	mustache	fiddles
dinosaurs	seeds	video	muscles	

Verbs About Cooking

sauté	chop	slice	cut	heat
boil	marinate	stir	taste	bake
fry	whip	scoop		

Next, she suggests combining nouns and verbs to see what interesting images develop. Here are a few of her combinations from the list above: "Dinosaurs marinate in the earth. The fiddles boiled the air with their music. The lilacs sliced the sky into purple."

To try this for yourself, create three sentences by matching three of the random nouns with three interesting verbs from the two lists below.

Random List of Nouns

baby	dancer	camper	ghost hunter
detective	ice skater	boxer	gambler
army general	guitarist	singer	scientist
stuntman	matador	skier	

Verbs That Describe Animal Movements

glided	stalked	swooped	dove	propelled
darted	fluttered	paddled	circled	slid
climbed	leaped	swung	jumped	flew
soared	scurried	wallowed	rolled	stomped

Consider adding some *-ing* participles to your sentences, using the animal movement verbs. In addition to the main verb you select, you might add one or two participles such as "Leaping, rolling, sliding" and so on. Participle brush strokes are created out of verbs and add to the action of a passage. Come prepared to share the best one of your three sentences in class. (Your teacher will set the point value for this bonus option if he or she decides to offer it.)

ACTIVITY 3 Paint by Zooming

▶ On the back side of this sheet, rewrite each of the following sentences, replacing the highlighted abstract nouns and verbs with more specific words. Then, using the list of prepositions on page 67 of this book, add a prepositional phrase to each of the ten sentences. Note that there are two words to revise in each sentence.

1 The grandmother **walked** into the **store.**

2 The general **touched** the **weapon**.

3 The **dog** ate his Alpo.

4 A **fish** **hit** the June Bug lure.

5 Teenagers **love** the **singer**.

6 The **object** **fell** on the floor.

7 The chimpanzee **jumped** onto the **thing**.

8 The morning sun **appeared** behind the **building**.

9 The **creature** **ate** my new Nike Air Jordans.

10 The **person** **talked** about performing in a band.

TIP With the verbs, you might want to use a thesaurus for ideas. With the nouns, you will need to think of "types." For example, with the word *dog*, you might enter *types of dogs* in Google.

Name ______________________________ Period __________

ACTIVITY 3 Paint by Zooming *continued*

1 ____

2 ____

3 ____

4 ____

5 ____

6 ____

7 ____

8 ____

9 ____

10 ____

Layering with Brush Strokes, Prepositional Phrases, and Adjectives

Writers also use a technique called **layering**. Layering means adding specific details using adjectives, prepositional phrases, and brush strokes. Along with zooming in on nouns and verbs, layering can make a passage even more powerful. Below (boldfaced and color coded) are the five types of layering techniques that can be used with any passage. Here are some suggested layering ideas for the paraglider passage that was revised earlier.

1 **Participle Brush Strokes** (an *-ing* word or phrase) **lumbering like some giant polar bear**

2 **Absolute Brush Strokes** (a noun and an *-ing* word or phrase) **hands clutching the guide wires**

3 **Adjectives Out-of-Order** (two adjectives shifted after a noun) **powerful and relentless**

4 **Appositives** (a noun that means the same thing as the noun before it) paraglider, **a novice**

5 **Prepositional Phrases** (a preposition followed by modifiers and a noun) **in the Andes Mountain Range**

Notice how each of these five layering techniques constructs a specific image that enhances the scene.

Layering with a Participle Brush Stroke

Down the steep slope the paraglider sprinted. The updraft thrust him forward and lifted him above the jagged peaks. Suddenly, where he had hoped to land, the clouds cloaked the ledge, **lumbering like some giant polar bear**, and the paraglider panicked.

Layering with an Absolute Brush Stroke

Down the steep slope the paraglider sprinted. The updraft thrust him forward and lifted him above the jagged peaks. Suddenly, where he had hoped to land, the clouds cloaked the ledge, lumbering like some giant polar bear. Hands clutching the guide wires, the paraglider panicked.

Layering with an Adjectives Out-of-Order Brush Stroke

Down the steep slope the paraglider sprinted. The updraft, **powerful and relentless,** thrust him forward and lifted him above the jagged peaks. Suddenly, where he had hoped to land, the clouds cloaked the ledge, lumbering like some giant polar bear. Hands clutching the guide wires, the paraglider panicked.

Layering with an Appositive Brush Stroke

Down the steep slope the paraglider sprinted. The updraft, powerful and relentless, thrust him forward and lifted him above the jagged peaks. Suddenly, where he had hoped to land, the clouds cloaked the ledge, lumbering like some giant polar bear. Hands clutching the guide wires, the paraglider, **a novice,** panicked.

Layering with a Prepositional Phrase

Down the steep slope **in the Andes Mountain Range**, the paraglider sprinted. The updraft, powerful and relentless, thrust him forward and lifted him above the jagged peaks. Suddenly, where he had hoped to land, the clouds cloaked the ledge, lumbering like some giant polar bear. Hands clutching the guide wires, the paraglider, a novice, panicked.

TIP It is important to realize that every type of layering isn't necessary in a passage. You can create powerful images by using just a few of the five layering techniques. The final paragraph shown on this page was purposely overloaded to show you how zooming and layering work.

Here is another example of zooming and layering. In this example, the author used zooming with all of the nouns and verbs, but selected just a few layering techniques to use.

Rough Draft

Thinking the **fish was** dead in a sling, and not noticing the slight vibrating **movement**, the **man held** the **rope** around the creature's **mouth** and **went** in close for a **picture**.

In the rough draft above, all the nouns (in blue) and verbs (in red) can be replaced with more specific images. Notice, in the examples on the next page, how the author zooms in.

Zooming in on Nouns (and Adjectives)

Thinking the **2000-pound great white shark was** dead in a sling, and not noticing the slight vibrating **twitch**, the **sport fisherman held** the **bull rope** around the creature's upper jaw and **went** in close for a **snapshot**.

Zooming in on Verbs

Thinking the **2000-pound great white shark hung** dead in a **sling**, and not noticing the slight vibrating **twitch**, the sport fisherman **grasped** the **bull rope** around the creature's **upper jaw** and **stepped** in close for a **snapshot**.

Layering with a Participle Brush Stroke

Thinking the 2000-pound great white shark hung dead in a sling, and **not noticing the slight vibrating twitch**, the sport fisherman grasped the bull rope around the creature's upper jaw and stepped in close for a snapshot. (Participles were already included.)

Layering with an Appositive

Thinking the 2000-pound great white shark hung dead in a sling, and not noticing the slight vibrating twitch, the sport fisherman grasped the bull rope around the creature's upper jaw and stepped in close for a snapshot, **a picture his family would sadly remember.**

Layering with a Prepositional Phrase

Thinking the 2000-pound great white shark hung dead in a sling, and not noticing the slight vibrating twitch **of its 3,000 knife-like teeth**, the sport fisherman grasped the bull rope around the creature's upper jaw and stepped in close for a snapshot, a picture his family would sadly remember.

ACTIVITY 4   Revise by Zooming and Layering

▶ Revise each sentence below by first zooming and then layering, using the examples on the previous pages as models. Begin by zooming in on just the nouns (in blue type) and verbs (marked in red) and replacing them with more specific words. After completing each sentence by zooming, revise by layering.

Revise by Zooming

Sentence 1 The **thing went** across the **water** and **moved** past the **place.**

_____

_____

Revise by Layering

▶ Next, layer over the revised sentence above by adding any two brush strokes and a prepositional phrase.

_____

_____

_____

_____

_____

_____

ACTIVITY 4 Revise by Zooming and Layering *continued*

▶ As you did with sentence 1 on the previous page, zoom in on the nouns and verbs marked with red and blue type in sentence two and replace them with specific examples.

Sentence 2 The **object came** into the earth's atmosphere and **went** down to the **area**.

_____

_____

▶ Next, layer over the revised sentence above a combination of any two brush strokes and a prepositional phrase.

_____

_____

_____

_____

_____

TIP Test your adjectives to be sure they are on a low level of abstraction. Picture the adjective in your mind. Does it paint a detail or does it simply label with an abstract term? General adjectives like *beautiful, wonderful, loving,* and *strange,* for example, are not visual. Use visual adjectives such as *furry, red,* and *wrinkled.*

Bonus Option From a favorite novel or nonfiction book, locate a sentence or two that contain examples of zooming and layering. Write your sentences on notebook paper and put your name and period at the top of the page.

ACTIVITY 5   Revise by Zooming and Layering

▶ Below is a photo of a woman making a jump at an equestrian competition where rider and horse are trained to leap a variety of barriers in the quickest time possible. On your own paper, write a short descriptive paragraph of the rider and horse. After you have completed your paragraph, revise by first zooming and then layering. From the five types of layering techniques, use only two in your paragraph and label each one in the margin. Finally, copy your final draft onto the next page.

ACTIVITY 5 ## Paint by Zooming and Layering *continued*

Final Draft

_____

_____

_____

_____

_____

_____

_____

_____

_____

_____

_____

_____

_____

_____

Creating Humor

In addition to zooming and layering, there are two additional ways in which specific images are used: (1) to create humor and (2) to create similes. The last part of this section shows humorous examples of how confusion can occur when specific images are replaced with abstract words that few people understand.

Using Specific Images

The next time you hear a comedian give a monologue, listen for the use of specific images. First, the comedian will give a straight line containing no humor. Then he or she will follow with a punchline that paints a very funny specific image. See how this works as you view the examples in the PowerPoint presentation your teacher shows.

Bonus Option Locate one joke that begins with a generalization and ends with a specific image. Underline or boldface the specific image. Remember that not every joke follows this pattern, but many do. Also, be sure your selection is appropriate for sharing.

Using Similes

At some time or other you have been told that a simile is a figure of speech in which two essentially unlike things are compared, usually in a phrase introduced by the word *like* or *as*. However, you may not know about the role of the image in a simile.

Writers create similes in the same way comedians create jokes. With comedians, the first part of a sentence is a setup for the second part, which provides the specific image. With similes, the words before *like* or *as* act as a setup for the second part of the sentence, which also provides a specific image. Unlike a joke, a simile may or may not create a comic image. Your teacher will show you some examples on PowerPoint, but here are a few to start you thinking:

It was as difficult as an elephant trying to pick up a pea.

—H.G. Wells

His teeth looked like a picket fence in a slum neighborhood.

—Stephen King

The voices were like a chorus of frogs on a spring evening.

—D.H. Lawrence

It was as dark as the inside of a magician's hat.

—Robert Campbell

Using Abstract Words to Imply the Opposite Meaning

Bill Gavin of *Mad Magazine* illustrated how little-known abstract words can be used to imply the opposite of what the abstract words actually mean. Here is a sample from his "Guaranteed Political Smear Speech." Following these excerpts are definitions for the abstract words he used, showing what the abstract words actually mean.

My fellow citizens, it is an honor and a pleasure to be here today. My opponent has openly admitted he feels an **affinity** toward your city, but I happen to like this area. It might be a **salubrious** place to him, but to me it is one of the nation's most delightful garden spots.

When I embarked upon this political campaign, I hoped that it could be conducted on a high level and that my opponent would be willing to stick to the issues. Unfortunately, he has decided to be **tractable** instead— to indulge in **unequivocal** language, to **eschew** the use of outright lies in his speeches, and even to make repeated **veracious** statements about me.

At first I tried to ignore these **scrupulous, untarnished fidelities.** Now I will do so no longer. If my opponent wants a fight, he's going to get one!

—*Mad Magazine*, #139, December 1970

To read the entire speech, go to http://www.mendosa.com/politics.html, http://people.ku.edu/~dadams/politico.htm

Abstract Word	Definition with Specific Meaning
affinity	a natural liking for something
salubrious	healthful
tractable	agreeable
unequivocal	clear
eschew	avoid
veracious	truthful
scrupulous	honest
untarnished	faultless
fidelities	loyalties

Strategies for the Grammar of Conventions

If you were searching for a business manager to operate a business you owned, would you hire the character telling the story in Andy Griffith's humorous monologue, entitled "What It Was, Was Football!" Read it on the next few pages, make a decision, and be prepared to explain why you would or wouldn't hire this individual.

It was back last October, I believe it was. We was a-goin' t' hold a tent service in this college town. And we got thar about dinnertime on Saturday.

And different ones of us thought that we ought to get us a mouthful to eat before that we set up the tent. And so, we got down off of the truck . . .

. . . and followed this little bunch of people through this small patch of woods. And we come up on a big sign, says, "Get somethin' t' eat chyere!"

And I went up and got me two hot dogs and a big orange drink. And before I could take a-ry mouthful of that food, this whole raft of people come up . . .

. . . And they got me t' where I couldn't eat nothin' up-like, and I dropped my big orange drink! . . . *I did!*

Well, friends, they commence to move, and thar warn't so much that I could do but move with 'em . . . through all kinds o' doors an' gates an' what-all!

102

And I looked up over one of 'em, and it says "North Gate." And we kept on a-goin', and purty soon we come up on a boy, and he says, "Ticket, please!"

And I says, "Friend, I don't have a ticket! I don't even know where it is that I'm a-goin'!" . . . *I did.*

Well, he says, "Come out as quick as y'can!" And I says, "I'll do 'er! I'll turn aroun' the first chanct I get!"

CONTINUED ON NEXT PAGE

Well, we kep' on a-movin' through thar, and soon everybody got where they was a-goin', because they parted, and I could see pretty good! . . . *I could!*

And what I seen was this whole raft o' people a-settin' on these two banks, and a-lookin' at one-another across this pretty little green cow pasture. . . .Well, *they was!*

And somebody had took and drawed white lines all over it, and drove posts in it, and I don't know what-all! . . . *They had!*

And I looked down thar, and I seen 5 or 6 convicts a-runnin' up and down, and a-blowin' whistles! . . . *They was!*

And I seen these purty girls a-wearin' these little-bitty short dresses, and a-dancin' around. So I sat down t'see what was a-goin' t' happen! . . . *I did!*

About the time I got sat down good, I looked down and I seen 30 or 40 men come a-runnin' out one end of a great big outhouse down there! . . . *They did!*

And everybody where I was a-settin' they got up and hollered. And about that time, 30 or 40 come a-runnin' out the other end of that outhouse.

And the other bankful, *they* got up and hollered. And I asked this feller that was a-settin' beside me, "Friend, what is it that they're a-hollerin' for?"

Well, he whup me on the back, an' he says, "Buddy, have a drink!" "Well," I says, "I believe I will have another big orange!" And I got it! . . . *I did!*

And when I sat back down, I seen that them men had got in two little-bitty bunches down thar! . . . *They had!* Real close! And they voted! . . . *They did!*

They elected one man apiece, and them two men come out in the middle of that cow pasture and shook hands like they hadn't seen one-another in a long time.

And then a convict come over to where the two of 'em was a-standin', and he took out a quarter, and they commence to "odd-man" right thar! . . . *They did!*

And then I seen what it *was* they was odd-manin' *for!* It was that both them bunchesful of men wanted this funny-lookin' little *punkin'* to play with!

They did! And I know they couldn't-a *eat* it, friends, 'cause they kicked it the whole evenin', and it never *busted!*

Anyway, what I was a-tellin' was both bunchesful wanted that thing, and one bunch got it! And it made the other bunch just as *mad* as they could *be!*

105

And, friends, I seen that evenin' the awfulest fight that I have ever seen in my life ! They'd run at one-another, an' kick one-another, an' th'ow one-another down, an' stomp on one-another, an' grind their feet in one-another, an' I don't know what-all! And just as fast as one of 'em 'd get hurt, they'd tote him off and run another one on . . .

Well, they done that as long as I set thar. But pretty soon this boy that had said "Ticket, please!," he come up to me, an' he says, "Friend, you're gonna have t' leave because it is that you don't have a ticket!" An' I says, "Well, all right!" And I got up and left! . . . *I did!*

And I don't know, friends, to this day what it was that they was a-doin' down thar! But I have studied about it. And I think that it's some kindly of a contest where they see which bunchful of them men can take that punkin' an' run from one end of that cow pasture to the other, without either gettin' knocked down . . . or *steppin' in somethin'!*

How much did grammar influence your decision about hiring the character that was describing the football game? If you are like most people, you probably assumed that the character's poor grammar signaled a lack of intelligence. However, language patterns are learned. Children learn to speak English from parents, siblings, and friends. When people make grammatical errors, it doesn't mean they are unintelligent. It only means their language has been shaped by the environment in which they were raised. There are many extremely intelligent and knowledgeable individuals who simply have learned patterns that educated society members consider incorrect.

However, the problem is that most educated people believe that correct grammar *does* imply intellect. Consequently, the way you write and speak affects your being hired for certain jobs, being admitted to colleges, being encouraged to join certain social groups and so forth. If you doubt this, consider what writers do if they want a character in a book, television program, or screenplay to look unintelligent. They have the character speak using poor grammar. So, Rocky in *Rocky I* says, "I wanted to prove I **weren't no** bum." In *American Gangster,* the character Frank remarks, "I **didn't** see **nothing**." The cashier in *Dumb and Dumber* says, "They **was** on their way to Rhode Island."

Notice how Mark Twain portrays Huckleberry Finn by having him make statements like these:

> When we **was** passing by the kitchen I fell over a root and made a noise.

> **There is** ways to keep off some kinds of bad luck, but this wasn't one of them.

> He got so he **wouldn't hardly** notice the others.

> I never **seen** anybody but lied one time or another.

> Tom and **me** found the money that the robbers hid in the cave.

> Then I **set** down in a chair by the window and tried to think of something cheerful, but it **warn't** no use.

In the novel we soon realize Huck is intelligent, but readers then assume he is not well educated, another misconception. Huck is not well educated in the traditional sense. His education is what we might characterize today as "street smart." In this section, we are going to learn what is wrong with the boldfaced words above and how to eliminate these errors.

How to Correct 91.5 percent of All Your Errors

Surprisingly, language scientists have shown that only 20 items account for 91.5 percent of all errors in student writing. In this section of the Activity book, you are going to examine a number of these critical errors.

However, to make this easy for you, we will be using a strategy called the "Express Line Checkout," an idea suggested by authors Jeff Anderson and Rei Noguchi. The express line checkout is similar to a grocery store checkout where you can quickly check out four or five items. Here you will be checking out four or five grammatical issues. So you will only need to learn a few concepts at a time. The checkout will involve (1) editing a short passage to show that you understand the grammatical ideas covered, (2) providing the correct words in sample sentences, or (3) creating your own passages to demonstrate your knowledge.

With this first concept you will check out by showing that you know the four types of problems that can occur with subject-verb agreement.

Concept A: Subject-Verb Agreement

1. Common Confusion
2. Inserted Prepositional Phrase
3. Pronoun as Subject and Object
4. Expletive Problem (There)

1. Subject-Verb Agreement: Common Confusion

Common confusion refers to an error that occurs with subject and verb side by side. More than any other agreement error, this one is often ranked as the worst type of error to make.

The rule: If the subject of a sentence is ONE person, place, thing, or idea, then use a singular verb. If there are MULTIPLE subjects, use a plural verb.

Notice how the subjects and verbs are paired in these correct examples:

The **plane is** an experimental model.

The **flames were** swallowing the house.

Bengal **tigers are** becoming extinct.

He was a very creative individual.

The **cat is** sleeping.

We were at the game.

The **bottle was** empty.

Here are a few more examples taken from the writings of well-known authors. As in all of the original author examples, the incorrect versions have been altered to illustrate an error, while the correct examples duplicate the author's actual statement.

✓**Incorrect** She **were** crawling on her belly through the mud. Brown clay-filled earth sucked at her hands as she pulled herself along.

★**Correct** She **was** crawling on her belly through the mud. Brown clay-filled earth sucked at her hands as she pulled herself along.

—Rebecca Tingle, *The Edge of the Sword*

✓**Incorrect** Mr. and Mrs. K **was** not old. They had the fair, brownish skin of the true Martian, the yellow coin eyes, the soft musical voices.

★**Correct** Mr. and Mrs. K **were** not old. They had the fair, brownish skin of the true Martian, the yellow coin eyes, the soft musical voices.

—Ray Bradbury, *The Martian Chronicles*

TIP Plural subjects follow the same rule. So, in sentences like "Fishing and hunting *are* popular sports in Alaska," the word *are* should be used. The words *fishing and hunting* represent more than one.

Painting Portraits with *Being* Verbs

You won't find many *being* verbs (*is, are, was, were, am,* and other forms of *be*) when an author is describing action because *being* verbs slow the motion in a scene. That is why professional writers emphasize the importance of using as many action verbs as possible. However, for character descriptions with little or no action, *being* verbs work well. Notice how in this character sketch from *The Sundowners* by Jon Cleary the being verbs give you a series of still shots.

> He **was** the color of the countryside. Dust **was** a dry skin on his face and forearms, but he **was** unaware of it. He had traveled so many roads, had eaten and breathed dust. Had it meant anything to him? His eyes, beneath the broad brim of his ancient hat, **were** closed almost shut against the glare of the road, but he missed nothing.

In this second example, Howard Pyle freezes the image of the Earl of Mackworth in his novel *Men of Iron*. The image Pyle creates is comparable to a portrait painting that captures a frozen moment for artistic effect.

> He **was** a tall man, taller than Myles's father. He had a thin face, deep-set bushy eyebrows and a hawk nose. His upper lip **was** clean shaven, but from his chin a flowing beard of iron-gray hung nearly to his waist. He **was** clad in a riding-gown of black velvet that hung a little lower than the knee, trimmed with otter fur.

Notice how Madeline L'Engle uses *being* verbs to create a portrait of Mrs. Whatsit in *A Wrinkle in Time:*

> After a few moments that seemed like forever to Meg, Mrs. Murry came back in, holding the door open for . . . **was** it the tramp? It seemed small for Meg's idea of a tramp. The age or sex **was** impossible to tell, for it **was** completely bundled up in clothes. Several scarves of assorted colors **were** tied about the head, and a man's felt hat perched atop. A shocking pink stole **was** knotted about a rough overcoat, and black rubber boots covered the feet.

Imitate the use of *was* and *were* in the examples above by describing the soldier on the next page. Create three or four sentences using at least two correct examples of *was* and one correct example of *were*.

ACTIVITY 1 Express Line Checkout

▶ Create three or four sentences using at least two correct examples of the verb *was* and one example of the verb *were*. Also, as a review, add two brush strokes to your description and label them in the margin. For help, refer to the examples of brush strokes you used in Section 1 of the Activity book. Write your sentences on the next page.

TIP Keep in mind that if the subject of a sentence is ONE person, place, thing, or idea, then use a singular verb. If there are MULTIPLE subjects, use a plural verb. Review the examples shown earlier.

ACTIVITY 1 Express Line Checkout *continued*

Subject-Verb Agreement: Common Confusion

_____

_____

_____

_____

_____

_____

_____

_____

_____

_____

_____

_____

_____

2. Subject-Verb Agreement: Inserted Prepositional Phrase

✓**Incorrect** **Each** of the soldiers **were** well-trained.

What you hear can deceive you. The combination of the words *soldiers were* sounds right, but the inserted prepositional phrase "of the soldiers" causes confusion. The subject is *Each* (not *soldiers*), which is singular, and you need to connect it with the singular verb *was*. Here is the correct version:

★**Correct** **Each** of the soldiers **was** well-trained.

✓**Incorrect** **Every one** of the five leading cars **were** in the wreck.

★**Correct** **Every one** of the five leading cars **was** in the wreck.

✓**Incorrect** **None** of the players **were** happy.

★**Correct** **None** of the players **was** happy.

Think of *none* as translating into *not one*. This might help you to hear the correct verb as in, "Not one of the players was happy."

TIP Double-check sentences that use *every, everyone, every one, each, each one, any, anyone,* and *none* to find the verb they connect with.

113

3. Subject-Verb Agreement: Pronoun as Subject and as Object

Pronoun as Subject

Here are the pronouns designated for use as the subject of a sentence: *I, you, she, he, it, we, you,* and *they.* Pronouns that are subjects fit into one of these two slots:

_____ was (or were) there.

It is (or are) _____.

Again, what you hear may deceive you. Because so many people use the incorrect form "It's him," "It is he" may sound incorrect. Here are a few examples of correct and incorrect use of pronouns.

> ✓**Incorrect** **It is him. The winner is her.**
> ⭐**Correct** **It is he. The winner is she.**

> ✓**Incorrect** **Him is it. Her is the winner.**
> ⭐**Correct** **He is it. She is the winner.**

TIP To check for the correct pronoun when a *being* verb is used, reverse the sentence. The correct version should sound more normal. Compare the pairs of sentences above.

Pronoun as Object

Six pronouns fit the objective slots: *me, her, him, it, us,* and *them.* Pronouns are objective when they fit in positions like these:

The pit bull was near _____.

The cat scratched _____.

Notice how the six object pronouns fit in the slots above: "The pit bull was **near me.** The cat **scratched her.**" The objective pronouns usually follow a preposition or an action verb. When you are uncertain which pronoun to choose, use the slots as a guide.

A tricky example occurs when a name is inserted as in these examples:

> ✓**Incorrect** Lebron handed the tickets **to Emiliano** and **I.**
> ⭐**Correct** Lebron handed he tickets **to Emiliano** and **me.**

> ✓**Incorrect** Grandpa told the rags-to-riches story of quarterback Johnny Unitas **to Roberto** and **I.**
> ⭐**Correct** Grandpa told the rags-to-riches story of quarterback Johnny Unitas **to Roberto** and **me.**

If this confuses you, just pretend there is only one person receiving the action. For example, notice how much easier it would be to pick the right pronoun if the last sentence read, **"Grandpa told the rags-to-riches story of quarterback Johnny Unitas to me."**

4. Subject-Verb Agreement: The Expletive Problem (*There*)

The expletive *there* is a false subject. The real subject comes later in the sentence. For example, notice how you might be tricked by the sentence, "There's bees in the nest." The subject is *bees*, not *There's*. This type of confusion has made the expletive problem one of the most common errors among even well-educated individuals. It is not unusual to hear television commentators use an incorrect expression like, "There's a number of things they need to do."

To avoid this problem change *there's* to the words *there is*. You should be able to recognize the error in the sentence, "There is fans waiting in line." If you can't recognize this error, try eliminating *there is* and juggling the sentence so the main noun comes first. For example, with "There is fans waiting in line," eliminate *there is* and place *fans* first so your sentence reads "Fans *are* waiting in line." Here are a few incorrect and corrected examples:

✓**Incorrect** There's many **reasons** why we can't go.

(**There's** is a contraction for **There is**. So the sentence incorrectly reads "**There is** many **reasons** why we can't go.")

⋆ **Correct** There are many **reasons** why we can't go.

(The word **reasons** is the subject.)

✓**Incorrect** There's hundreds of books on art.

(**There's** is a contraction for **There is**. So the sentence incorrectly reads "**There is** hundreds of books on art.")

⋆ **Correct** There are hundreds of books on art.

Quick Self Review

Look at each of the sentences below and mark them *C* correct or *I* incorrect. Also, circle the subject of each sentence except in sentences where the pronoun is determined by a preposition. In those, circle the preposition. This is a self test. Once you have marked your answers, you can check on the previous pages to see if you are correct. Seven of the ten sentences are there and the other three sentences are close examples. With items you missed, review the previous explanations. This should help prepare you for the express line checkout that follows.

_____ 1. It is him.

_____ 2. LeBron handed he tickets to Emiliano and me.

_____ 3. Each of the soldiers was well-trained.

_____ 4. None of the players were happy.

_____ 5. There's many reasons why we can't go.

_____ 6. Every one of the five leading cars was in the wreck.

_____ 7. Grandpa told the rags-to-riches story of quarterback Johhny Unitas to Roberto and I.

_____ 8. The winner is her.

_____ 9. Anna, one of the key players, were outstanding.

_____ 10. We was at the game.

ACTIVITY 2 Express Line Checkout

Subject-Verb Agreement

▶ Examine the passage below and try to find the seven subject-verb agreement errors. Circle each one you locate. Then on the next page write (A) the noun or pronoun subject that goes with the verb, (B) the incorrect verb, and (C) the correct verb. Each answer should look something like this (A) *surfers* (B) *was* (C) *were*. If you find an example of *there's* that is incorrect, simply write (B) *there's* and (C) *there are*. Also, if the subject is incorrect, mark your answer with (A) subject, (B) verb, and (C) correct subject.

Poachers Killing Gorillas and Chimps for Bush Meat Delicacy

In Central Africa, some of man's favorite animals is being pushed close to extinction by two disturbing trends—civilization's appetite for luxury foods and desire for virgin timber. Here, in the space of two days, an entire family of gorillas were shot and killed—three adult females, two babies, and the father, a big silverback.

The gorillas was killed to be butchered, smoked, and sold in the markets of Cameroon as "bush meat," an increasingly popular food. "The slaughter of chimpanzees and gorillas is absolutely diabolical. My colleagues and me can't imagine that this can go on much longer before these animals are extinct," warns Richard Leakey with the Kenya Wildlife Service.

But in Central Africa, the commercial trade in bush meat continues to grow. There's many problems. Markets teem with meat from many forest animals, including endangered chimpanzees, gorillas, and elephants—not as necessary protein sources but as delicacies.

Also, unrestrained logging, mostly by European companies, has hurt these primates. Each of these lumber companies are driving new access roads into old-growth forests, making the proliferation possible. Roads now penetrate deep into areas once inaccessible to hunters. "Both hunting and logging is at the core of the problem," says Randy Hayes of the Rainforest Action Network.

—Gary Streiker, CNN Correspondent

ACTIVITY 2 Express Line Checkout *continued*

(A) Noun or Pronoun Subject	(B) Incorrect Verb	(C) Correct Verb
1 (A)_____	(B)_____	(C)_____ .
2 (A)_____	(B)_____	(C)_____ .
3 (A)_____	(B)_____	(C)_____ .
4 (A)_____	(B)_____	(C)_____ .
5 (A)_____	(B)_____	(C)_____ .
6 (A)_____	(B)_____	(C)_____ .
7 (A)_____	(B)_____	(C)_____ .

Note Errors were added to the original excerpt for the exercise. The original can be found in the online article "Poachers Killing Gorillas, Chimps for Bush Meat Delicacy" by Gary Streiker, CNN Correspondent. Go to http://www.cnn.com/TECH/science/9812/30/africa.bushmeat/.

Concept B: Avoiding Sentence Fragments

1. Avoiding a Participial Phrase Fragment

2. Avoiding a Subordinate Clause Fragment

3. Avoiding a Prepositional Phrase Fragment

4. Avoiding a Relative Pronoun Clause Fragment

The test of a fragment is to read it out loud. Imagine that a friend just walked up to you and said, "Walking down the road." You might ask, "Walking down the road what?" Fragments leave you puzzled. They are incomplete and need to be attached to a sentence to make sense. Unlike fragments, sentences complete a thought as in, "Walking down the road, my uncle spotted Bigfoot." Your mind recognizes a complete thought. While the statement might create some interesting discussion, it doesn't leave you confused about its meaning.

Sentence fragments are often like icebergs that break off from a glacier. If you look at a fragment and the sentences before and after it, you can often see how the fragment might have once been attached. Examine the following four structures that can become fragments when not attached to a sentence.

1. Sentence Fragment Created with a Participial Phrase

✓**Incorrect** I was six years old when King Nicander came to the island of my birth. **Demanding tribute and a hostage.**

⋆**Correct** I was six years old when King Nicander came to the island of my birth, **demanding tribute and a hostage.**

—Caroline Cooney, *Goddess of Yesterday*

2. Sentence Fragment Created with a Subordinate Conjunction

✓**Incorrect** A sense of humor is what makes you laugh at something. **Although it would make you mad if it happened to you.**

⋆**Correct** A sense of humor is what makes you laugh at something, **although it would make you mad if it happened to you.**

—Mark Twain

3. Sentence Fragment Created with a Prepositional Phrase

✓**Incorrect** According to the Gemological Institute of America, India was the only source of diamonds in the world. **Until the 1730s.**

★**Correct** According to the Gemological Institute of America, India was the only source of diamonds in the world **until the 1730s.**

4. Sentence Fragment Created with a Relative Pronoun Clause

✓**Incorrect** Vincent Van Gogh was a famous artist. Who only sold one of his paintings.

★**Correct** Vincent Van Gogh was a famous artist **who only sold one of his paintings**.

If you use a fragment and your artistic intent isn't obvious and appropriate, your teacher will no doubt mark it as an error. So it is best to avoid all fragments in assigned papers. Using fragments correctly is a difficult task.

Concept C: Avoiding Colliding Sentences

1. Run-on Sentence   3. Fused Sentence

2. Comma Splice   4. *However*

NOTE Authors play with words and sometimes use fragments purposely. Here is one example that uses fragments to create the feeling of confusion that a headache brings:

Hand shaking him. Making his head roll on his neck. Terrible headache. Thudding, shooting pains. —Stephen King, *Firestarter*

There are several ways to correctly punctuate two consecutive sentences: (1) with a period after the first sentence and a capital letter starting the second sentence, (2) with a comma and the word *and*, (3) with a semicolon, (4) with a subordinate conjunction at the beginning of the first sentence and a comma before the second sentence, and (5) with the subordinate conjunction after a comma between the two sentences. Here are some contrasting examples of what happens when these methods are used and not used.

1. Run-on Sentence

A run-on joins two or more sentences with only a coordinating conjunction (*and, but, or, nor, for*). The writer leaves out the comma needed with the conjunction to join two sentences. See the incorrect example that follows.

✓**Incorrect** I will not bring sheep to **class and nerve** gas is not a toy.

★**Correct** I will not bring sheep to **class, and nerve** gas is not a toy.

★**Also Correct** I will not bring sheep to **class; nerve** gas is not a toy.

The average sentence length of a popular magazine article runs between 15 and 20 words. To locate run-on sentences and comma splices in your writing, search for sentences longer than 20 words. Don't count each sentence word by

120

word. Simply survey your writing for sentences that seem long. Then read each suspected sentence aloud and listen for your natural pauses because that will be a sign that punctuation is needed.

2. Comma Splice

A comma splice incorrectly joins two sentences with only a comma as in the example below.

> ✓**Incorrect** They're working on cars powered by fuel made from **beans, you** think you hate getting behind a bus now?

> ★ **Correct** They're working on cars powered by fuel made from **beans. You** think you hate getting behind a bus now?

> —Jay Leno monologue

3. Fused Sentence

A fused sentence runs two sentences together without any punctuation in between. The example below illustrates this:

> ✓**Incorrect** The next morning I slept **late around** eleven I was awakened by a muffled bang.

> ★ **Correct** The next morning I slept **late. Around** eleven I was awakened by a muffled bang.

> —Lan Samantha Chang, "Housepainting"

4. *However*

The word *however* does not join sentences. It must have a semicolon with it when located between sentences. "However" is an interrupter like "furthermore." Here is an example:

> ✓**Incorrect** Did you ever notice when you blow in a dog's face, he gets mad at you**, however,** when you take him in a car, he sticks his head out the window.

> ★ **Correct** Did you ever notice when you blow in a dog's face, he gets mad at you**; however,** when you take him in a car, he sticks his head out the window.

> —Jerry Seinfield monologue

TIP *However* cannot join two sentences without the help of a semicolon.

121

In the correct example on the previous page, a semicolon is used with *however* to join the second sentence. In the example below, a period is used with *however* to join the two sentences.

> ★**Correct** Did you ever notice when you blow in a dog's face, he gets mad at you. **However,** when you take him in a car, he sticks his head out the window.

The word *however* can be dropped into the middle of one sentence. In this case, it is set off with commas as in this example:

> ★**Correct** An acre of trees, **however,** can remove about 13 tons of dust and gases every year from the surrounding environment.

A Review of Five Ways to Punctuate Two Sentences

For the next activity, you will need to review the five ways of joining sentences to create your own descriptions using what you've learned. Notice how the same two sentences from Harry Harrison's *A Stainless Steel Rat Is Born* can be punctuated in five different ways.

(1) Use a period after the first sentence and a capital letter starting the second sentence.

I approached the front door of the First Bank of Bit O' Heaven. **It** sensed my presence and swung open with an automatic welcome.

(2) Use a comma and the word *and*. (You must have both.)

I approached the front door of the First Bank of Bit O' Heaven, **and** it sensed my presence and swung open with an automatic welcome.

(3) Use a semicolon.

I approached the front door of the First Bank of Bit O' Heaven; it sensed my presence and swung open with an automatic welcome.

(4) Use a subordinate conjunction at the beginning of the first sentence and a comma before the second.

When I approached the front door of the First Bank of Bit O' Heaven, it sensed my presence and swung open with an automatic welcome.

(5) Place the subordinate conjunction after a comma between the two sentences.

I approached the front door of the First Bank of Bit O' Heaven, **when** it sensed my presence and swung open with an automatic welcome.

ACTIVITY 3 Express Line Checkout

Five Ways to Punctuate Sentences

▶ Select one of the two images below and create a two-paragraph description about it. Include in your paragraphs one example of each of these methods of punctuating two sentences: (1) a period after the first sentence and a capital letter starting the second sentence. (2) a comma and the word *and*, (3) a subordinate conjunction at the beginning of a sentence and a comma in between sentences, (4) a comma and a subordinate conjunction in between two sentences, and (5) a semicolon. Label each example in the margin by marking the number of the method you are using and by drawing a line to it.

Bonus Option

Add to your paragraphs examples of two different brush strokes. Label these as well and earn bonus points for each correct brush stroke.

123

ACTIVITY 3 Express Line Checkout *continued*

_____

_____

_____

_____

_____

_____

_____

_____

_____

_____

_____

_____

ACTIVITY 4 Express Line Checkout

Editing for Fragments, Run-on Sentences, Comma Splices, and Fused Sentences

▶ Locate the six sentence errors in this altered passage taken from *Wanda Hickey's Night of Golden Memories* by Jean Shepherd. Complete the answer sheet on the following page in two ways. For fragments list the first word of the fragments on the first line and list the type of error (fragment) on the second line. For other errors—run-ons, comma splices, and fused sentences—list the word before the place where a period is needed even if a comma occupies that spot. On the second line, identify the type of error as a run-on, comma splice, or fused sentence.

"You going to the prom?" asked Schwartz, as we chewed on our salami sandwiches under the stands of the football field.

"Yep, I guess so," I answered as coolly as I could.

"Who ya taken'?" Flick joined in the discussion. Slurping at a bottle of Nehi orange.

"I don't know. I was thinking of Daphne Bigelow." I had dropped the name of the most spectacular girl in the entire high school. If not the state of Indiana itself.

"No kidding!" Schwartz reacted in a tone of proper awe and respect, tinged with disbelief.

"Yeh. I figure I'd give her a break."

Flick snorted, the gassy orange pop going down the wrong pipe. He coughed and wheezed brokenly for several moments I had once dated Daphne Bigelow, and although the occasion, as faithful readers will recall, was not a riotous success, I felt that I was still in the running. Several occasions in the past month had led me to believe that I was making a comeback with Daphne. Twice she had distinctly acknowledged my presence in the halls between classes, once she actually spoke to me.

"Oh, hi there, Fred," she had said in that musical voice.

"Uh . . . hi, Daph," I had replied wittily. The fact that my name is not Fred is neither here nor there, she had spoken to me. She had remembered my face. From somewhere.

ACTIVITY 4 Express Line Checkout *continued*

Word or Words Around the Period or Comma	Type of Error
1 _____	_____
2 _____	_____
3 _____	_____
4 _____	_____
5 _____	_____
6 _____	_____

Concept D: Avoiding Word Confusion

This section deals with homonyms—words that sound alike but are spelled differently and have different meanings. There are over 300 pairs of such words, and most rarely cause a problem in writing. Pairs like *hair* and *hare*, *plain* and *plane*, *cents* and *scents* seldom create confusion. A few homonyms, however, are troublesome. We will look at four groups of these words.

1. *There, Their,* and *They're*

Suppose you are proofreading a paragraph, and this sentence appears: "**They're** house was cold." Follow three steps.

(1) Substitute *They are* and see if the sentence makes sense. In this case the sentence would read "**They are** house was cold," which doesn't make sense. Go to the second step.

(2) Ask yourself if the word **their** can be used to show ownership. **Their** always describes a noun, and that noun is usually located one to three words right after it. In our example, the word **house** comes right after **their,** and the word **their** implies that the house belongs to someone. So, this is correct: "**Their** house was cold."

A simple check that usually works is to substitute **my** in the sentence and see if it reads well. **My** and **their** can fit in the same slot. For example, you could say "**My** house was cold," indicating that **their** would also be correct.

(3) Now if the sentence you are looking at doesn't fit the checks in steps one and two, almost certainly you need the word **there,** but how can you be sure? The word **there** always points to a person, place, thing, or idea as in the following: There is the mailman. There is a great idea. There is the place to buy a quadruple dip butterscotch milkshake. The word **there** points to nouns. So "Their house was cold" is the correct choice. Here is another example for you to study.

Matthias struggled to his feet. He fought his way back into the crowd, squeezed through a doorway and along the hall. Suddenly, fresh air hit his face, and

_____ was sunlight.

—Margaret Peterson Haddix, *Among the Enemy*

2. *Your* and *You're*

This problem only requires one step. **You're** can always be replaced with **you are**. If you've written **you're**, try substituting **you are**. If it doesn't work, then the correct word is **your**. For example, suppose you have written the sentence, "Is that _____ shoe? If you place **you are** in the slot, it reads, "Is that **you are** shoe." So you know the correct word should be **your**. Compare the correct and incorrect examples that follow.

✓**Incorrect** Is that snake **you're** pet?

★**Correct** Is that snake **your** pet?

✓**Incorrect** The word is that this Miurata villain will dock in the harbor sometime tomorrow, maybe mid-noon. **Your** safe enough here, though.

★**Correct** The word is that this Miurata villain will dock in the harbor sometime tomorrow, maybe mid-noon. **You're** safe enough here, though.

—Istrani Wolves, *Voyage of Slaves*

✓**Incorrect** Shhh, **your** gonna wake the kids.

★**Correct** Shhh, **you're** gonna wake the kids.

—From the film script *Finding Nemo*

ACTIVITY 5 Express Line Checkout

There, Their, and They're

▶ Complete each of the sentences below by filling in the blanks with *there, their,* or *they're.*

1 _____ is a great place to live.

2 Do you think _____ gone?

3 _____ is no reason to act that way.

4 _____ are mice in the attic.

5 _____ coming to the party.

6 They can't make up _____ minds.

7 I know _____ considering exploring the cave.

8 He said _____ dog was dangerous.

9 I don't know _____ names.

10 I think _____ house is haunted.

ACTIVITY 6 Express Line Checkout

Your and *You're*

▶ Correctly insert *your* or *you're* in each of the following sentences.

1 _____ a very creative individual.

2 Let me know if _____ going to the movie.

3 It's _____ turn.

4 Is that _____ cat on the roof?

5 I hope _____ able to come tomorrow.

6 Malcolm saw _____ CD in lost and found.

7 _____ eyes are a deep brown.

8 Share _____ book with Jacquelyn.

9 Who is _____ choice?

10 Jo says _____ feeling better today.

11 _____ a good artist.

12 What is _____ favorite song?

3. *It's, Its*

As with the confusion of *your* and *you're,* the problem with *it's* and *its* takes only one step to proofread. Simply remember that *it's* is short for *it is,* and *its* means ownership. So when faced with a choice like "*Its* or *It's* crawling up your back," substitute *It is* to see if the sentence still makes sense. Here is how this would read: "*It is* crawling up your back." The sentence reads clearly, so the word *It's* is correct. Try not to be confused by the fact that both *Its* and *It's* sound the same. In writing, they differ.

If you are faced with a choice in a sentence like, "*It's* or *Its* leg was hurt," use the same approach that you did in the last example. Substitute *It is* to see if that fits. Here is how this second example would read: "*It is* leg was hurt." So *Its* is correct and works when *It is* doesn't. The word *its* shows ownership. Here are a few examples of both correct and incorrect uses:

✓**Incorrect** **Its** a small world after all. **Its** a small world after all. **Its** a small world after all.

★**Correct** **It's** a small world after all. **It's** a small world after all. **It's** a small world after all.

—Richard M. Sherman and Robert B. Sherman

✓**Incorrect** Workers dropped hammers, spilled paint, stumbled over each other and occasionally pulled brown paper bags from their pockets and took quick gulps from hidden bottles. "**Its** like watching a Marx Brothers' movie," said Eugene Rouleau, the barber.

★**Correct** Workers dropped hammers, spilled paint, stumbled over each other and occasionally pulled brown paper bags from their pockets and took quick gulps from hidden bottles. "**It's** like watching a Marx Brothers' movie," said Eugene Rouleau, the barber.

—Robert Cormier, *Heroes*

✓**Incorrect** He could smell the decomposing cow as the Boa opened **it's** mouth and dislocated **it's** jaws in order to seize him.

★**Correct** He could smell the decomposing cow as the Boa opened **its** mouth and dislocated **its** jaws in order to seize him.

—Geraldine McCaughrean, *The Stones Are Hatching*

4. Sit, Sat, Set

Sit means to rest.

Sit down and relax.

Sat is something that already has happened.

She **sat** here yesterday.

Set can be replaced with the word put.

Set the book on the table.

Solving the *Sit, Sat, Set* Problem

Here is how to solve the **sit, sat, set** problem. Imagine that you have a sentence like, "_____the glass on the table," and you are uncertain which word to use. First, test for the word **put. Put** can only replace the word **set.** So like a detective, you need to place **put** in the sentence and see if that works. In this case it does. "Put the glass on the table" works. So "**Set** the glass on the table" is correct. To **set** means to place something or to arrange something.

TIP One exception to the replacement of *put* for *set* is when the word *set* means to arrange as in "Please set the table." This doesn't occur nearly as often as the use of *set* for *put*, but you should be aware of this.

If **put** does not work in a sentence like, "_____ down and have some cake," you will need to make a choice between **sit** and **sat**. To decide, keep in mind that **sat** describes something that has already happened, as in "Bombo **sat** in that rocking chair last week." **Sit** means to rest by moving into a chair or into a restful place, as in "Our cat likes to **sit** on the window seat." If you keep these two definitions in mind, you should know that "Sit down and have some cake," is correct.

ACTIVITY 7 Express Line Checkout

Sit, Sat, Set

▶ Fill the blanks in the following ten sentences with *sit, sat,* or *set.*

1 Only Sue can _____ still for three hours.

2 Tonya _____ her book on the table.

3 The eagle _____ on her nest.

4 Deron _____ in Uncle Wilber's chair.

5 I watched our dog _____ by the fire.

6 Last night Monk _____ on his new rug.

7 The parrot _____ on Blackbeard's shoulder.

8 The fisherman _____ his fish in the cooler.

9 The elephant _____ on the trainer's hat.

10 Otis _____ the turkey on the table.

ACTIVITY 8 Express Line Checkout

Their, They're, There, Your, You're, It's, Its, Sit, Sat, Set

▶ This passage is adapted with added errors from "Adventure Dog" by Dave Barry. The answer sheet for this activity on page 136 has three sets of lines. On line one write the incorrect word. On line two write the first word that follows it. On line three write the correct word choice. There are ten incorrect words.

Excerpt from "Adventure Dog"

I have this idea for a new television series. It would be a realistic action show, patterned not after you're imaginary dog, but after the true-life experiences of my dog, Earnest. The name of the show would be "Adventure Dog." The theme song would go:

Adventure dog,

Adventure dooooooogggg

Kind a big, kind a strong

Stupid as a log.

You're typical episode would be about an exciting true adventure that happened to Earnest. For example, here's the script for an episode entitled: "Adventure Dog Wakes Up and Goes Outside."

It is 6:17 A.M. Adventure Dog is sleeping in the hall on it's rug. Suddenly she hears a sound. Her head snaps up. Somebody is up! Time to swing into action! Adventure Dog races down the hall and, skidding on it's four paws, turns into the bathroom, where to her total shock, she finds: The Master, whom she has not seen since LAST NIGHT! YAYYYYYY!!

ADVENTURE DOG: Bark!

MASTER: SET DOWN!

ACTIVITY 8 **Express Line Checkout** *continued*

Now Adventure Dog bounds to the front door, in case the Master is going to take her outside. Their is a slim chance. He has only taken her outside for the past 2,637 consecutive mornings. But just in case, Adventure Dog is ready.

ADVENTURE DOG: Bark!

Can it be? Yes! This is unbelievable! The Master is coming to the door! Looks like Adventure Dog is going outside! YAAAYYY!

MASTER: SET DOWN!

Now the Master has opened the door approximately one inch.

Adventure Dog realizes that, at this rate, it may take the Master a full three-tenths of a second to open the door all the way. This is bad. He needs help. Adventure Dog alertly puts her nose in the crack and applies 600,000 pounds of force to the door.

MASTER: HEY!

DOOR: WHAM!

And now Adventure Dog is through the door, looking left, looking right, her finely honed senses absorbing every detail of the environment, every nuance and subtlety, looking for . . . Holy Smoke! They're it is! Its the YARD! Right in the exact same place it was yesterday! Its turning out to be an UNBELIEVABLE adventure!

— Dave Barry, "Adventure Dog"

Note Errors were added to the original excerpt for this exercise. The original can be found in Dave Barry's book, *Dave Barry's Greatest Hits*.

ACTIVITY 8 Express Line Checkout *continued*

Incorrect Word	Word After	Correct Word
1 _____	_____	_____
2 _____	_____	_____
3 _____	_____	_____
4 _____	_____	_____
5 _____	_____	_____
6 _____	_____	_____
7 _____	_____	_____
8 _____	_____	_____
9 _____	_____	_____
10 _____	_____	_____

ACTIVITY 9 Express Line Checkout

Their, They're, There   Your, You're   It's, Its   Sit, Sat, Set

▶ Your task in this exercise will be to create an imaginary conversation in which two people are discussing who might own an unusual object they have found together. The object might actually belong to one of the individuals, or it might belong to someone else. The two characters could be discussing its ownership.

Another possibility might be that the object is an antique from the distant past or a strange item left by aliens from another world. Similarly, the conversation might be an argument or a joint analysis. Perhaps one person knows about the object, but doesn't want the other person to know. Let your imagination play with the possibilities.

In your one- to two-paragraph discussion, include one correct example from each of the four types of word confusions: (1) **Their, They're, There,** (2) **Your, You're,** (3) **It's, Its,** and (4) **Sit, Sat, Set.** Label each item you use correctly in the margin. You will find some possibilities for characters on the next page. Write your paragraphs on pages 139 and 140.

Bonus Option Add three brush strokes in your description of the two characters.

Conversation, Daniel Nevins, 1995

Some Sample Characters to Consider

an inventor and a magician

a pirate and a parrot

a marine sergeant and his four-year-old daughter

a gunfighter and an Indian maiden

a business woman and a spy

a queen and a tourist

a student and the principal

a millionaire and a professional gambler

a thief and a minister

a quarterback and a coach

a doctor and a prison inmate

a mad scientist and a talking frog

a police office and a reporter

an alien and a big game hunter

a brain surgeon and her patient

an artist and a robot

a detective and a teenager

a grandmother and a professional wrestler

If none of the suggested character combinations appeals to you, create two characters of your own or use the elderly woman and the magician shown below.

ACTIVITY 9 Express Line Checkout *continued*

_____

_____

_____

_____

_____

_____

_____

_____

_____

_____

_____

_____

ACTIVITY 9 **Express Line Checkout** *continued*

_____

_____

_____

_____

_____

_____

_____

_____

_____

_____

_____

_____

_____

Concept E: Mixed Problems

1. Double Negatives

2. Restrictive and Nonrestrictive Clauses

3. Incorrect Punctuation of Appositive Brush Strokes

4. Incorrect Punctuation of Adjectives Out-of-Order

1. Double Negatives

A *double negative* occurs is when a writer or speaker places two negative words in the same sentence as in the following:

It **didn't never** act like it was a wild animal.

The words **didn't** and **never** create confusion with some readers. In the minds of some readers, the two negatives create a positive. So **did not never** to some readers means **always.** Educated individuals recognize the double negative as a significant error. For anyone seeking a job that requires a good communicator, avoiding double negatives is important. To avoid double negatives, examine your writing for combinations of these negatives:

no, not, none, no one, nothing, nowhere, neither, nobody, never, doesn't, isn't, wasn't, wouldn't, couldn't, shouldn't, won't, can't, don't, hardly.

Be especially aware of common combinations like "don't do nothing," "wasn't nobody," and "couldn't never."

Here are some examples to review:

✓**Incorrect** I **never** saw **nothing**.

★ **Correct** I saw **nothing**.

✓**Incorrect** He **wasn't nobody** I knew.

★ **Correct** He **was nobody** I knew.

✓**Incorrect** She **doesn't never** vote.

★ **Correct** She **doesn't** vote.

One tricky example of a negative is the word *hardly*. This is considered a negative even though it doesn't have the letter **n** like other negatives. Here is an example of a common error:

✓**Incorrect** I **couldn't hardly** speak.

★ **Correct** I **couldn't** speak.

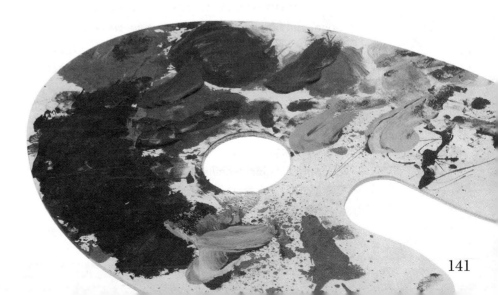

2. Restrictive and Nonrestrictive Clauses

A *restrictive clause* is one that is essential to the meaning of a sentence. For example, examine the sentence, "The pit bull **that has rabies** is sleeping in our house." The information provided by "that has rabies" is essential to the meaning of the sentence. This important clause is labeled as *restrictive* and is not set off with commas because it is important information.

By contrast, a nonrestrictive clause adds secondary information—information that isn't absolutely necessary to the meaning of the sentence. For example, in the sentence, "The pit bull, **which is an interesting creature**, is sleeping in our house," the information expressed in "which is an interesting creature" isn't essential. If the sentence is read without this clause, the most important information remains. So the clause is considered nonrestrictive and is set off with commas because it is information that isn't absolutely needed.

Both restrictive and nonrestrictive clauses describe a noun, and both begin with *who, whom, whose, which,* or *that.* Here are two correct examples—one of a restrictive adjective clause and one of a nonrestrictive adjective clause. Notice how the restrictive clause describing the word *chimpanzees* provides an important modification of the meaning. Without *that are sent into space,* the sentence loses its meaning. The nonrestrictive clause in the second example adds incidental, unimportant information.

Restrictive Chimpanzees **that are sent into space** become taller.

Nonrestrictive Ants can carry twenty times their own body weight, **which is useful information if you're moving and you need help carrying a potato chip across town.**

—Ron Darian

Many grammar books say that the word *that* should be used with restrictive clauses and *which* with nonrestrictive clauses. But in the past few years, writers have been using these two words interchangeably. Since usage patterns sometimes change, it is a good possibility that the older rule with these two words will eventually be replaced. However, for clarity, use *that* for restrictive clauses and *which* for nonrestrictive clauses, as in these examples:

Restrictive The chess set **that was valued at over 10 million dollars** is called the jewel royale.

Nonrestrictive Our cat, **which is a lot like my grandpa,** spends about 70% of his day sleeping.

Notice how the boldfaced clause in the restrictive example contains important information, while the clause in the nonrestrictive example contains incidental information. The word *which* and the commas that set it off indicate a nonrestrictive clause.

3. Appositive Brush Strokes
4. Adjectives Out-of-Order

Two additional nonrestrictive structures are used to enrich images: appositive brush strokes and adjectives out-of-order. These two structures seldom cause a problem, but keep in mind that both are set off with commas, indicating a zoom lens revealing added detail. While the added detail is not essential, it often adds to the power of the descriptive image. Here are a few examples to refresh your memories.

Appositives

The elephant, **an angry 1200-pound beast,** charged the lions.

The newborn harp seal, **a tiny creature with milk-white fur,** nestled in the snow.

Adjectives Out-of-Order

The **angry** elephant, **monstrous and fierce,** charged the lions.

The **tiny** kitten, **horrified and shaken,** suddenly realized that he was not cuddling next to his mother.

Note For further examples, review Painting with Brush Strokes in Section 1.

To complete the activity on page 145, examine the altered passage below from "Best Witches from Slats" by Mike Royko looking for errors in double negatives, restrictive and nonrestrictive clauses, appositive brush strokes, and adjectives out-of-order.

Slats Grobnik our fifteen-year-old neighbor didn't never care much for Halloween. It made him angry that all the kids in the neighborhood went around soaping windows, tipping over garbage cans, and leaping out of gangways to scare old ladies.

That's the way he acted all year, and it was no fun when everybody else did it.

Slats Grobnik smart but devilish didn't like going to no parties either.

"All they do is tell Halloween stories about witches on brooms," he sneered. He said he would rather go to the tavern with Beer Belly Frank Grobnik his uncle. "At least Uncle Frank tells stories about fishing," he said.

Slats did attend one party. His mother insisted he accept an invitation from a boy in the Fairlawn neighborhood which is where some people owned their own houses.

"I want to wear a costume so nobody doesn't recognize me," Slats said.

"All you gotta do is wash your face for that," his father said.

His mother who wanted Slats to go suggested he dress up like a bum, and Slats asked how bums dress. After she told him, he looked at his father and said, "You got anything that'll fit me?"

ACTIVITY 10 Express Line Checkout

▶ On the first line of the answer sheet, list the word or words that are in error. On the second line, identify the error as (1) a double negative, (2) a restrictive or nonrestrictive clause, (3) two missing commas—one before and one after an appositive brush stroke, or (4) two missing commas—one before and one after adjectives out-of-order. You should find eight errors.

Word or Words in Error	**Type of Error**
1 _____	_____
2 _____	_____
3 _____	_____
4 _____	_____
5 _____	_____
6 _____	_____
7 _____	_____
8 _____	_____

Concept F: Avoiding Brush Stroke and Parallel Structure Errors

1. Dangling Participle
2. Lack of Parallel Structure
3. Comma after an Introductory Element
4. Commas in a Series

If you have worked through the brush strokes in Section 1 and the musical elements in Section 2, you have already practiced the skills you'll need for this part of the book. In this section, the focus will be on errors that might occur using brush strokes and parallel structures.

1. Dangling Participle

If your participle brush stroke isn't located close to the noun you are painting, the meaning of the sentence can be jumbled, sometimes with comic effect:

> **Strolling hand in hand to the barn,** three young bulls charged the farmer and his wife.

> **Racing from the escaped chimps,** the wallet fell from the zookeeper's pocket.

In these sentences, the highlighted participle phrases modify the noun right after it. So the first example reads like the bulls are strolling hand in hand. Similarly, the second sentence reads like the wallet was racing from the chimps. To correct a dangling participle, move the participle brush stroke close to the word it modifies as in these examples:

> **Strolling hand in hand to the barn,** the farmer and his wife were charged by two young bulls.

> **Racing from the escaped chimps,** the zookeeper lost his wallet.

When using a participle brush stroke, think of your brush stroke as a way of zooming in for a close-up view. The image you create should add close-up details of the noun you are describing and should be located close to it. "**Strolling hand in hand to the barn,**" is close to *the farmer and his wife*. "**Racing from the escaped chimps**" is close to the word *zookeeper*.

2. Lack of Parallel Structure

As you may recall from Section 2 on musical rhythms, parallel structures involve repetitions of almost every grammatical structure: nouns, verbs, adjectives, adverbs, prepositional phrases, participial phrases, relative pronouns, and clauses. The better you are able to recognize structures, the easier it will be for you to hear them and create them. If you have difficulty understanding parallel structure, review "The Musical Rhythms of Language" (Section 2), and visit http://www.americanrhetoric.com/figures/parallelism.htm for a few excellent examples.

Parallel structures create a powerful rhythm in sentences. However, when a powerful rhythm is started and then broken, it is considered an error in parallelism. For example, compare these two sentences. The first correctly uses parallel structure. The second breaks the rhythm.

★ **Correct** Jose enjoys **swimming, fishing, and hiking.**

✓ <u>**Incorrect**</u> Jose enjoys **swimming, fishing, and to hike.**

This is the most common type of error with parallel structures, and it occurs because the writer doesn't hear the rhythm. As you read, listen for rhythms and imitate them in your own writing. Here are a few examples to help you learn to listen to the music of parallel structures. Once you begin to hear these rhythms, you will be able to experiment with them in your writing.

Melodic Rhythm

Councilmen, I stand before you today not only as your Queen: **I come to you as a** mother; **I come to you as a** wife; **I come to you as** a Spartan woman; **I come to you** with great humility.

—From the film script *300*

Broken Rhythm

Councilmen, I stand before you today not only as your Queen: **I come to you as a** mother and as a wife, and of course, as a Spartan woman too. Also, **I come** with great humility.

Melodic Rhythm

All right **who did it**? **Who did it**? You are going to stand sweating at those battle stations until someone confesses. And I'm going to find out **who did it** if it takes all night. Roberts! That's the one. **Get him up here. Get him up here** right now. **Get him up here**!

—From the film script *Mr. Roberts*

Broken Rhythm

All right **who did it**? You are going to stand sweating at those battle stations until someone confesses. And I'm going to find out who is responsible if it takes all night. Roberts! That's the one. **Get him up here** right now. And make it fast because I'm angry.

ACTIVITY 11 Express Line Checkout

Parallel Structure

▶ The passage on the right is taken from the film *Miracle*. At this point, Coach Herb Brooks is trying to inspire his team before they play for the Olympic hockey championship against the powerful Russian team. To excite his players, he uses parallel structures, repeating words and phrases until the team charges out of the locker room, determined to win.

▶ Begin by reading the entire passage and listening for the rhythms and repetitions the coach uses. Then go back and circle each word that repeats. You should end up circling 43 different places where words are repeated. Keep in mind that each word in a repeated phrase counts individually as part of the 43. There are actually only 14 different words repeated in different places to create the total of 43.

From the film *Miracle*

Great moments are born from great opportunity, and that's what you have here tonight, boys. That's what you've earned here, tonight. One game. If we played them ten times, they might win nine. But not this game. Not tonight.

Tonight, we skate with them. Tonight, we stay with them, and we shut them down because we can! Tonight, we are the greatest hockey team in the world. You were born to be hockey players—every one of you.

And you were meant to be here tonight. This is your time. Their time—is done. It's over. I'm sick and tired of hearing about what a great hockey team the Soviets have. This is your time!! Now go out there and take it!

—From the film script *Miracle*

Note The complete original speech can be found in the screenplay for *Miracle*. To hear the full speech from the film, go to the Web site American Rhetoric at http://www.americanrhetoric.com/MovieSpeeches/moviespeechmiracle1.html

3. Comma after an Introductory Element

In this section, rather than showing an incorrect sentence with the comma missing, only the correct example will be displayed. The idea is to emphasize the grammatically correct use of use of the comma with introductory (1) words, (2) phrases, and (3) clauses.

Single Introductory Word

When a sentence is introduced with a single word, the word is usually an adverb and often ends in "ly." Some typical introductory words include *quickly, ironically, suddenly, sadly, finally, yesterday, yet, still, however, nonetheless,* and *often.* Adverbs like these, which begin a sentence, should be set off with a comma. To determine if you have a one word introductory element, eliminate the word. Then, see if the sentence still makes sense. Examine these two examples:

⋆ **Correct Ironically,** Garrett's mother was a guidance counselor at Trace Middle.

—Carl Hiaasen, *Hoot*

⋆ **Correct Suddenly,** the club car rattle-banged by, a dozen volcanic faces with fiery eyes crushed close to the windows, fists hammering the glass.

—Ray Bradbury, "Night Train to Babylon"

Long Introductory Prepositional Phrase

When a sentence begins with a long prepositional phrase, the phrase is set off with a comma. Notice the punctuation in these sentences:

⋆ **Correct In the far north of the Alaskan Yukon,** folks learned quickly that cats are smarter than dogs. You can't get eight cats to pull a sled through the snow.

—Jeff Valdez monologue

⋆ **Correct By the time we got back to the barn with Bets and her new bull calf,** I felt I was in a dream, fuzzy around the edges.

—Gary Paulsen, *Popcorn Days and Buttermilk Nights*

Short Introductory Prepositional Phrase

With short prepositional phrases—one less than five words—the writer has the option of omitting the comma. In these sentences the authors could have decided to omit or include the comma. Each decided differently.

> ⋆ **Correct With Robin in the lead,** the werewolves surged over the rail.
>
> —L.A. Meyer, *Under the Jolly Roger*

> ⋆ **Correct At last** it was over. The players thronged backstage, laughing and talking.
>
> —Sarah Thomson, *The Secret of the Rose*

Introductory Participle Brush Stroke (Phrase)

When a participle brush stroke begins a sentence, it is always set off with a comma. Here are a few examples:

> ⋆ **Correct Pulling the Remington from its saddle scabbard,** Dodge held the reins in his teeth while he lever-cocked his rifle.
>
> —Robert Newton Peck, *The Horse Hunters*

> ⋆ **Correct Snapping my arm forward,** I winged a stone toward the woods. It fell short of Ripley Power's dog, Tyrus.
>
> —Karen Hesse, *Phoenix Rising*

To feel the power of participle brush strokes, you may want to review "Painting with Brush Strokes" (Section 1). Also, to better understand subordinate conjunctions, review "The Musical Rhythms of Language" (Section 2).

Introductory Clause with a Subordinate Conjunction

Subordinate conjunctions create clauses that connect to main sentences. The subordinate conjunction requires a companion comma to make this connection. In the examples below, the subordinate conjunction *as* combines with the comma after the word *last* to join the boldfaced clause to the main sentence. In the second example, the subordinate conjunction *When* combines with the comma after *bullets* to join the boldfaced clause to the main sentence. Each subordinate conjunction works with a comma to correctly attach to the sentence.

> ⋆ **Correct As he approached the summit of the hill at last,** something began to happen. He was not warmer. If anything, he felt more numb and more cold.
>
> —Lois Lowry

> ⋆ **Correct When assaulted again by bullets,** the men burst out a barbaric cry of rage and pain.
>
> —Stephen Crane, *The Red Badge of Courage*

4. Commas in a Series

Use commas to separate words, phrases, or clauses in a series. When you have several items in a series, place a comma after each item except the last. If the word *and* precedes the last item, there should be a comma before the word *and*. For example, notice how this sentence is punctuated: "Fred caught a bass, a bluegill, and a pike." Here are more examples of words, phrases, and clauses in a series.

Words in a Series

★ **Correct** Shopping for a **backpack, sleeping bag, thermal tent, cooking pots, lights, and all the gear I needed** was half the fun.

—Harry Harrison, *A Stainless Steel Rat Is Born*

★ **Correct** After an hour or so, I met Dad at the door with **two Black Sabbath tapes, two very large speakers, and a bunch of speaker wire in hand.** He was carrying a **bunch of cables, some switches, a handful of gears that looked broken, and a test tube.**

—Adam Selzer, *How to Get Suspended and Influence People*

★ **Correct** Over the next several days they bartered the coffee by the half pound and by the nogginful to the neighbors, keeping back only ten pounds for their own use. When it was empty, they had taken in **a side of bacon, five bushels of Irish potatoes, four of sweet, a tin of baking powder, eight chickens, various baskets of squash, an old wheel and loom in need of minor repairs, six bushels of shell corn, and enough split shakes to reroof the smokehouse.**

—Charles Frazier, *Cold Mountain*

With commas used in a series, some grammarians argue that the comma before the conjunction (*and, or, for, nor, but, yet, so*) is optional, but by always including it, you can't go wrong.

Phrases in a Series

★ **Correct** Three passions have governed my life: **the longings for love, the search for knowledge, and pity for the suffering.**

—Bertrand Russell

★ **Correct** I have a dream that one day even the state of Mississippi, a state **sweltering with the heat of injustice, sweltering with the heat of oppression,** will be transformed into an oasis of freedom and justice . . . With this faith, we will be able **to work together, to pray together, to struggle together, to go to jail together, to stand up for freedom together,** knowing that we will be free one day.

—Martin Luther King, Jr., from "I Have a Dream"

Clauses in a Series

★ **Correct** As an American, I want to speak for those women in my own country, **women who are raising children on the minimum wage, women who can't afford health care or child care, women whose lives are threatened by violence, including violence in their own homes.**

—Hillary Rodham Clinton, from a speech at the U.N. 4th World Conference on Women

★ **Correct** You have to set standards for **how you work, how you treat others, how you let yourself be treated.**

—Cathy Guisewite

Note As in three of the four examples on this page, authors decided to omit the word *and*. This was done to make the rhythm more dramatic.

152

ACTIVITY 12   Express Line Checkout

Comma after an Introductory Element, Commas in a Series

The excerpt on the next page is taken from Douglas Adams' *The Hitchhiker's Guide to the Galaxy*. In this scene the two main characters—Arthur, the earthling, and Ford, the alien—discover that they are going to be shot into outer space and may die. At the same time the earth is about to be destroyed by a committee of aliens called the Galactic Hyperspace Planning Council. They are building a hyperspace express route for spaceships, and the earth is in the way.

Ford and Arthur survive, and that is how the novel begins. In the passage, Arthur mentions the words *mostly harmless*. Earlier he had found out that the only description of earth given in *The Hitchhiker's Guide to the Galaxy*, which catalogues all knowledge of the universe, consisted of two words *mostly harmless*.

Your task is to locate the nine errors in this altered passage. Each of the errors will match one of these two categories: (1) a missing comma after an introductory element or (2) missing commas in a series. Keep in mind that although the errors will be in only two categories, each category includes several different types of mistakes.

Most of the sentences need only one comma to correct them. With these simply write the word before the missing comma on line one of the answer sheet on page 155 and identify the type of comma error on line two as (1) a missing comma after an introductory element or (2) missing commas in a series.

With a couple of sentences—those with commas in a series—you might have two or three words that need a comma. For example, suppose your sentence was "The assignment is a strange mind-blowing weird and difficult activity." There should be a comma after three words: "The assignment is a **strange, mind-blowing, weird,** and difficult activity." Notice the comma before ***and.*** Your answer sheet would look something like this:

1. strange,   commas in a series

2. mind-blowing,   commas in a series

3. weird,   commas in a series

153

ACTIVITY 12   Express Line Checkout *continued*

Excerpt from *The Hitchhiker's Guide to the Galaxy*

"So . . . er, what happens next?" asked Arthur.

"Oh. Well. In a few moments in front of us on the far wall a hatchway will open automatically, and we will shoot out into deep space—I expect—and asphyxiate. If you take a lungful of air with you, you can last for up to thirty seconds, of course," said Ford.

Sticking his hands behind his back Ford's eyebrows raised. He started to hum an old Betelgeusian battle hymn. To Arthur's eyes he suddenly looked lost confused and hopeless.

'So this is it," said Arthur, "we are going to die."

"Yes," said Ford, "except . . ." No! Wait a minute!" Suddenly he lunged across the chamber at something behind Arthur's line of vision—possibly an escape hatch a warning button an oxygen unit. "What's this switch?" he cried.

"What? Where?" cried Arthur, twisting round.

"No, I was only fooling," said Ford. "We are going to die after all." Analyzing the problem he slumped against the wall again and carried on the tune from where he left off.

"You know," said Arthur, "it's at times like this, when I'm trapped in a Vogon airlock with a man from Betelgeuse and about to die of asphyxiation in deep space, that I really wish I'd listened to what my mother told me when I was young."

"Why, what did she tell you?"

"I don't know. I didn't listen."

"Oh." said Ford. Appearing calm yet defeated he carried on humming.

"This is terrific," Arthur thought to himself, "The earth has gone. McDonald's has gone. All that's left is me and the words *mostly harmless*. Any second now all that will be left is *mostly harmless*. And yesterday the planet seemed to be going so well."

A motor whirred. A slight hiss built into a deafening roar of rushing air as the outer hatchway opened onto an empty blackness studded with tiny, impossibly bright points of light. Ford and Arthur popped into outer space like corks from a toy gun.

Note Errors were added for the exercise. The original can be found in Douglas Adams' *The Hitchhiker's Guide to the Galaxy*, one of the very few humorous science fiction novels.

ACTIVITY 12 Express Line Checkout *continued*

Word Before Missing Comma	Type of Comma Error
1 _____	_____
2 _____	_____
3 _____	_____
4 _____	_____
5 _____	_____
6 _____	_____
7 _____	_____
8 _____	_____
9 _____	_____

ACTIVITY 13 Express Line Checkout

A Final Project

Musicians practice, experiment, and create before performing. Throughout this Activity book, you have gone through a similar process as a writer. The final project is an invitation to show what you've learned. With this activity, you will have to demonstrate your knowledge of various conventions and grammatical structures by using them in a description. You will need to follow four steps in this activity.

Step One: Create a Rough Draft
▶ On a piece of notebook paper, create two or three paragraphs describing one of these two images:

ACTIVITY 13 Express Line Checkout *continued*

Step 2: Revise with Seven Techniques

▶ Create a revision using the seven techniques in the checklist below. If you have already used some of these in your rough draft, you have saved some time since you won't have to create them as part of your revision. With each of the seven techniques, whether you created them in your rough draft or revision, you will need to label them in the margin of your final draft. Draw a line from each label to the word or words that illustrate that technique. You can review any techniques that you have forgotten in earlier sections of this Activity book

To be sure you have used all of the required techniques, use this checklist as a guide when labeling.

_____ 1 A Participle Brush Stroke

_____ 2 Adjectives Out-of-Order

_____ 3 An Absolute Brush Stroke

_____ 4 An Appositive Brush Stroke

_____ 5 Action Verbs (No more than three linking verbs)

_____ 6 Specific Nouns and Verbs Used

_____ 7 Parallel Structure

ACTIVITY 13 Express Line Checkout *continued*

Step 3: Editing for Common Errors

▶Proofread your description and review your paper for these five categories of errors. All of these errors are described in this section of this Activity book. You do not have to write anything in this step. Your job is simply to make sure you haven't made any of these common errors.

_____ 8 Sentence Fragments

_____ 9 Run-ons

_____ 10 Incorrect Use of Comma after an Introductory Element

_____ 11 Incorrect Use of Commas in a Series

_____ 12 Incorrect Use of Comma with a Restrictive Element

ACTIVITY 13 Express Line Checkout *continued*

The Final Draft

_____

_____

_____

_____

_____

_____

_____

_____

_____

_____

_____

_____

_____

ACTIVITY 13 **Express Line Checkout** *continued*

_____
_____
_____
_____
_____
_____
_____
_____
_____
_____
_____
_____
_____
_____
_____
_____

ACTIVITY 14 Just For Fun

Find the Celebrity Errors

▶ Almost everyone makes a grammatical error from time to time, and this can be embarrassing—especially if you are a well-known politician, a popular sportscaster, or newscaster with a national reputation. Just for fun, see if you can find the grammatical errors spoken by these well-known celebrities. Each sentence contains one error, and all of these errors have been taught in this program.

1   "I really didn't know him hardly at all." —Al Pacino

2   "There's only two people in the world you should lie to: the police and your girlfriend." —Jack Nicholson

3   "I found both the city and it's inhabitants warm and gracious." —Sienna Miller about Pittsburgh

4   "There are many parallels between my son and I. We both wear diapers. I don't have a problem, but I'm too lazy to go to the bathroom."
                                                                                        —Will Ferrell

5   "I didn't really meet hardly anyone who wasn't supportive of the film." —Forest Whitaker, on the people of Uganda's reaction to the production of *The Last King of Scotland*

6   "Rarely is the question asked, 'Is our children learning?'" —George W. Bush at a 2001 Washington TV/Radio Correspondents' dinner.

7   "A while back, him and the president came up with another solution." —Marty Delfin, reporter for the *San Juan Star* on National Public Radio

8   "There's always other frontiers." —Kanye West

9   "I cannot go no further." —Shakespeare

10   "Each animal has, like, their own space." —Paris Hilton, describing her collection of animals

Image Credits

various pages: iStock; 1 (top and bottom): © 2008 Jupiterimages Corporation; 2, 15, & 143: Natphotos/Digital Vision/Getty Images; 6: Photolibrary; 7: Daniel H. Bailey; 8: David Madison/Digital Vision/Getty Images; 11 & 143: Tom Brakefield/Digital Vision/Getty Images; 12: Digital Vision/Getty Images; 16: Tom Brakefield/Stockbyte/Getty Images; 17; Thomas Barwick/Digital Vision/Getty Images; 18: Tom Brakefield/Stockbyte/Getty Images; 21: Juan Silva/ Digital Vision/Getty Images; 22 & 143: Image Source/Fotosearch; 24: Karl Weatherly/Photodisc/Getty Images; 29: © 2008 Jupiterimages Corporation; 32 (left): Photodisc/Getty Images; 32 (right): Jeremy Woodhouse/Digital Vision/ Getty Images; 37: Stockbyte/Getty Images; 39: Alan Thornton/Stone/Getty Images; 51 (top): © 2008 Jupiterimages Corporation; 51 (bottom): iStock; 53: SuperStock; 57: SuperStock; 58: Image Asset Management/SuperStock; 60: Digital Vision/Superstock; 63: © Barnes Foundation/SuperStock; 64: iStock; 68: Brand X/SuperStock; 69: Digital Vision/Getty Images; 70 (left): Digital Vision/Getty Images; 70 (right): Stockbyte/Getty Images; 72: Harry R. Noden; 75: Harry R. Noden; 77: Heath Robbins/Photonica/Getty Images; 79 : Kurt Miller; 81 (top): © 2008 Jupiterimages Corporation; 81 (bottom): © 2008 Jupiterimages Corporation; 82: iStock; 83: iStock; 84: iStock; 85: iStock; 86: Greg Von Doersten/Getty; 87: iStock; 89: iStock; 92 & 93: iStock; 93 (right): Harry Noden; 97: Izzy Schwartz/Digital Vision/ Getty; 101 (top): © 2008 Jupiterimages Corporation; 101 (bottom): iStock; 102–106: "What It Was, Was Football" Images © 1958 Mad Magazine, E.C. Publications, Inc. Images courtest of Doug Gilford, madcoversite.com; 111: Nick Daly/Digital Vision/Getty; 113: BananaStock/SuperStock; 115: Lauren Nicole/Photographer's Choice/Getty; 123: (left) John Foxx/Stockbyte/Getty; 123 (right): Adam Crowley/Photodisc/Getty; 128: BananaStock/SuperStock; 132: Corbis/SuperStock; 137: Conversation 1995 © Daniel Nevins/SuperStock; 138 (left): Steve McAllister/Stockbyte/Getty; 138 (right): Joshua Ets-Hokin/Photodisc/Getty; 141: © 2008 Jupiterimages Corporation; 151: © 2008 Jupiterimages Corporation; 156 (left): Tom Brakefield/Digital Vision/Getty; 156 (right): Tom Brakefield/Digital Vision/Getty

Every reasonable effort has been made to properly acknowledge ownership of all material used. Any omissions or mistakes are unintentional and, if brought to the publisher's attention, will be corrected in future editions.